T0358192

Cambridge Elements ≡

Elements in New Religious Movements
Series Editor
Rebecca Moore
San Diego State University
Founding Editor
†James R. Lewis
Wuhan University

BLACK HEBREW ISRAELITES

Michael T. Miller

CAMBRIDGE
UNIVERSITY PRESS

Shaftesbury Road, Cambridge CB2 8EA, United Kingdom

One Liberty Plaza, 20th Floor, New York, NY 10006, USA

477 Williamstown Road, Port Melbourne, VIC 3207, Australia

314–321, 3rd Floor, Plot 3, Splendor Forum, Jasola District Centre, New Delhi – 110025, India

103 Penang Road, #05–06/07, Visioncrest Commercial, Singapore 238467

Cambridge University Press is part of Cambridge University Press & Assessment, a department of the University of Cambridge.

We share the University's mission to contribute to society through the pursuit of education, learning and research at the highest international levels of excellence.

www.cambridge.org
Information on this title: www.cambridge.org/9781009486989

DOI: 10.1017/9781009400107

When citing this work, please include a reference to the DOI 10.1017/9781009400107

First published 2024

A catalogue record for this publication is available from the British Library.

ISBN 978-1-009-48698-9 Hardback
ISBN 978-1-009-40008-4 Paperback
ISSN 2635-232X (online)
ISSN 2635-2311 (print)

Cambridge University Press & Assessment has no responsibility for the persistence or accuracy of URLs for external or third-party internet websites referred to in this publication and does not guarantee that any content on such websites is, or will remain, accurate or appropriate.

Black Hebrew Israelites

Elements in New Religious Movements

DOI: 10.1017/9781009400107
First published online: January 2024

Michael T. Miller
Author for correspondence: Michael T. Miller, Michael.miller@nym.hush.com

Abstract: The Black Hebrew Israelite (BHI) movement claims that African Americans are descendants of the ancient Israelites and it has slowly become a significant force in African American religion. This Element provides a general overview of the BHI movement, its diverse history/ies, ideologies, and practices. The Element shows how different factions and trends have taken the forefront at different periods over its 140-year history, leading to the current situation where diverse iterations of the movement exist alongside each other, sharing some core concepts while differing widely. In particular, the questions of how and why BHI has become a potent and attractive movement in recent years are addressed, arguing that it fulfills a specific religious need to do with identity and teleology, and represents a new and persistent form of Abrahamic religion.

Keywords: African American Religion, Black Judaism, American religions, Black Religion, Abrahamic religion

ISBNs: 9781009486989 (HB), 9781009400084 (PB), 9781009400107 (OC)
ISSNs: 2635-232X (online), 2635-2311 (print)

Contents

Introduction

Black Hebrew Israelism (BHI) is a new religious movement (NRM) which emerged in America in the twentieth century, although its roots go back to at least the nineteenth century. BHI is a broad umbrella, admitting many different groups of varying stances. The basic precept which all share is that African Americans are descended from the ancient Israelites, who were Black; some claim that they are the only authentic descendants, while some accept Rabbinic Jews as siblings, and some include other peoples such as Native Americans as Israelite descendants. Membership is thus largely African American, although it has spread gradually to other areas, and there are groups with international presence including in the Caribbean, Israel, the United Kingdom, and several African states. There are no reliable figures, but estimates for US membership range from 40,000 to 1.5 million.[1]

This Element is intended to serve as a compact introduction to BHI, its major players and groups, and their doctrines. It will also provide a simple path through the evolution of this multifarious and highly complex NRM. While much of the basic material is present in other texts, which should be consulted for more information and deeper analysis, there are new details which enrich our understanding and several figures that are presented and discussed here for the first time.

James Landing wrote:

> Black Judaism set the stage and strongly influenced the rise of Black Islam in [the US] and it is ideologically similar. Yet the movement of Black Judaism occupies no space in Afro-American history, is little recognised nor considered by their historians, and is still felt to be a fringe movement with little black community meaning or involvement. As one of the earliest black nationalist movements from which most sprang, it deserves better. (Landing 2002: 383).

The earliest scholarship, made up of scattered articles, chapters, and books during the twentieth century, contextualized BHI either as a Black Religion or as Judaism.[2] Locating it within these frames, it was usually seen as a strange and minor outgrowth, one which was sure to be short-lived, and of little influence; a temporary curiosity which was certain to disappear, albeit one worthy of recording while it existed. Since the end of the twentieth century, however, scholars have determined that BHI was not only an important and highly influential movement in Black America but that its legacy is still growing. BHI was an important part of the Black Nationalism of the early twentieth

---

[1] Extrapolated from Pew Research Center (2013) and LifeWay Research (2019), respectively.
[2] These texts can be found within the references of the texts discussed herein.

century and predated Black Islam as an expression of Black pride and separatism. It thus anticipated and contributed to the Afrocentric movement of the 1960s. During the twenty-first century, the movement has gone from a marginal one to claiming hundreds of thousands – perhaps millions – of members all over the United States and increasingly abroad, representatives of which can be seen on many inner-city street corners.

During the twenty-first century, the basic developmental history of BHI has been given a firm footing. James Landing (2002), in a book compiling decades of research into a treasure trove of detailed information from around the United States, showed that the roots of the first founders were within the Holiness movement.[3] Therefore American Christianity could be viewed as the origin point, and especially the trend toward Judaization with an emphasis on the Old Testament and "restoration" of Old Testament practices, which is evident in American Protestantism.

Jacob Dorman (2013) provided confirmation of the Holiness influence, while showing the complexity of the movement, demonstrating that it has consistently appropriated and creatively combined elements from many different traditions. Dorman has further shown that the evolution was not linear, but composed of distinct waves, which emphasized different qualities and brought new concepts into the movement at each stage. Thus, Dorman argues that the restorationist aspect is only one part of BHI; from its inception it has displayed a diverse interest in various elements of other traditions, combining them in such a way as to create something new which served the needs of Black Americans. Hence, Dorman rejects any notion that BHI comes from either Judaism or from Black Christianity; it is a new, bricoleur tradition, forged from the specific experiences and world of Black Americans.

In the earliest stages, leaders appeared to be attempting to return to a kind of Apostolic Christianity, free of the developments that had taken place within the institutional church. Later iterations moved decisively away from Christian concepts in their entirety, some seeking a closer alignment with contemporary Judaism, and some viewing the rabbinic traditions as no more authentic than the

---

[3] The Holiness movement was begun in the 1830s by the sisters Sarah Lankford and Phoebe Palmer, two New York Methodists who developed and taught the idea that holiness could be attained instantly, as a filling with the Holy Spirit. It quickly spread over the United States and attracted a lot of African Americans, especially as some Holiness churches taught racial equality; they also taught biblical literalism and sought to restore the Hebraic form of some rituals. As the movement developed, some came to believe that their sanctification could bring them perfect health and even immortality; and some began to adhere to the Mosaic laws, especially the dietary regulations. Many of these beliefs still exist in the later-wave BHI camps. Not only were Black preachers identifying with the Israelites, so were many whites at this time. Indeed, the end of the nineteenth century was populated with fascination with the Israelites, from these restorations of rituals and Apostolic Christianity to Anglo-Israelism.

Christian. Throughout its evolution, however, Black Hebrew Israelites (BHIs) have insisted on the ultimate veracity and dependability of the Bible, whether they included the New Testament as part of it or not. Prior scholarship had already shown the significance of the Old Testament for enslaved Africans and the ways in which identification with the Israelites formed an inspirational paradigm for their struggle (Raboteau 1978). In many groups, aspects described in the Bible (such as specifically named nations) are understood to be eternal truths which still exist today, leading to odd-seeming assertions such as the descent of Chinese and Japanese from Middle Eastern populations only some 3,000 years ago. For almost all BHIs, the Bible is the sole authoritative resource, containing all of history.

We can say that BHI, in all its diversity, emerged from a confluence of sources, including the identification of enslaved Africans with the biblical Israelites; mixed-race Jewish communities and families emerging especially from the Caribbean, who were aware of their Jewish heritage but either not accepted within the Jewish community or only partially accepted (Ben Ur 2020; Leibman 2021); and from a contemporaneous American fascination with the Israelites, including Anglo-Israelism that was especially present in the teachings and rituals of Freemasonic orders. There was also, as Dorman has shown, an orientalist fascination with distant cultures, which formed the basis for healers, magicians, and others, who added a layer of exoticness to their credentials by asserting their background and knowledge gained in far-off, Middle Eastern and Asian lands. Some of the religious entrepreneurs in New York were able to learn from recent Ashkenazi Jewish immigrants in order to bolster their assertions of Jewish identity.

While Landing and Dorman now provide the best historical constructions of the movement, the two best theoretical analyses remain unpublished doctoral theses. Andre Key has suggested that we must see BHI as a part of Black Religion, and principally as a manifestation of this theological approach, which in itself has always been eclectic and not bound by the doctrinal and historical restraints of the normative forms of either Christianity, Judaism, or Islam:

> Black Judaism shares certain core beliefs, mythologies, and theodicies with religious traditions in the African American community such as Black Islam, and certain manifestations of Black Christianity. [These are] religious orientations that can be referred to as *Black Religion*. The central tenet of *Black Religion* is the desire to combat racial oppression on divine terms with theologically-based anthropologies. *Black Religion* operates not as a single religious system but as a *plurifaith*, a collection of African American religious traditions undergirded by the concern with protecting, defending, and advocating for the full humanity and spirituality of African people. (Key 2011: 23; italics in original)

Key developed a typology for BHI groups, which I will refer to in this Element (Key 2011, 2014a). Articulating the dual nature of the BHI movement, Key defines the two axes by acceptance or rejection of, on one hand, the New Testament and African American Church, and on the other, normative Rabbinic Judaism. The result is four conceptual spaces (Figure 1): the Torah-Only groups (who refuse both the New Testament and Talmud); the Holiness groups, who reject rabbinic tradition but accept that of the Black Church; the rabbinic, who reject the Black Church but accept rabbinic tradition; and the Messianic who accept (to some degree) both. Of course, each group admits a unique perspective and admixture of different elements. In addition, we should add a Cultural Nationalist aspect, which foregrounds Afrocentric dress and thought, and cuts across the Messianic and Torah-only perspectives. It should be noted that all these groups prioritize the Hebrew Bible, taking either the New Testament or rabbinic tradition as an addition to the fundamental scriptural revelation. Arguably, this is what makes them Hebrew Israelites and prevents their absorption into the Black Church or Rabbinic Judaism. It should also be remembered that there is a large variety within these categories, but they are a useful framework for understanding the relationships between different groups.

Across all groups, however, Key writes: "Hebrew Israelites are attempting to accomplish three tasks: a) first reclaim a lost African identity, b) come to terms theologically with the involuntary presence of African people in the Americas,

	Rejection of Christianity/New Testament		
Accommodation of Rabbinic Judaism	Rabbinic	Torah-only	Rejection of Rabbinic Judaism
	Messianic	Holiness	
	Accommodation of (Black) Christianity/New Testament		

Figure 1 A visualization of Key's four elements

and c) articulate an understanding of the divine that supports their liberation." (Key 2011: 197). In the final section, we will see that some recent iterations actively reject African identity.

Key's thesis is an autoethnographic exploration, wherein he recounts his encounter and travel through Hebrew Israelite communities, beginning with the One West Camp, before joining Beth Shalom B'Nai Zaken Ethiopian Hebrew Congregation (EHC), and finally, almost, into Orthodox Judaism. Walter Isaac's doctoral dissertation, on the other hand, is a historical-philosophical treatise grounded in his heritage as a Black and Native American Hebrew Israelite. Isaac advances an overall critique of the approach of previous scholars, suggesting a new model which rejects "ontological Jewishness" entirely. Isaac shows the many areas through which Blacks (and Native Americans) could exist within and on the periphery of American Judaism, or have incorporated Judaism into their sense of self, and argues that the concept of Jewishness as a single determined property must be withdrawn. These "alternative understandings of Jewish identity and religious practice" (Isaac 2012: 64) on the part of African American Jews, could exist in three ways: First, some enslaved Africans could have come from tribes of Israelite descent. Second, some Sephardic or Ashkenazi Jewish slaveholders procreated with their enslaved women and sired biracial Jewish offspring. Finally, those enslaved by Jewish families were, to varying degrees, indoctrinated in Jewish traditions and *even if they were not converted* there were halakhic grounds for considering them Jewish upon manumission. Isaac argues that, because of this, the existing concept of a single, strictly determined Jewishness is flawed and cannot address the history of Black America. This means that there is a structural prejudice within the halakhic regulations such that the Jewish community finds it easier to accord Jewish status to the (legitimate/white-skinned) descendants of slaveholders than the descendants of enslaved, partly because records were kept less strictly in the case of the latter. As he puts it, "the important historical question is not, "Did Jewish slave owners convert their slaves?" Rather, it is "What did 'being/becoming Jewish' look like from the enslaved Africans' points of view'?" (Isaac 2012: 67). Thus, "one cannot only use concepts most appropriate for understanding Jewish slave masters in order to rigorously study and understand the social worlds of enslaved Africana Jewish peoples" (Isaac 2012: 70).

While Landing and Dorman offer sympathetic but necessarily outsider perspectives on the movement, Key and Isaac provide insider perspectives which are still scholarly. These are thus invaluable resources for interested scholars, although they have not received the open and extensive critical analysis that publication makes possible. Isaac's three pathways – and particularly the last two, for which there is direct evidence, especially in the Caribbean – should be added to those given above as possible backgrounds to individuals' assertions of Israelite identity.[4] However, we should remember that, since the BHI *movement* began, many have joined congregations simply for what those congregations offered them intellectually, socially, theologically, politically, and spiritually, without necessarily having any prior association with Judaism. That is, deciphering the origins of the movement can only go so far in understanding its subsequent and contemporary existence and significance.

Some of this significance could be expressed by saying that the BHIs present a new iteration of Abrahamic religion, one developed by the American underclass as part of their struggle for liberation. This is the underlying argument of this text: BHI is neither an iteration of Judaism nor Christianity, although at points the boundary between BHI and these faiths is near-invisible. The movement is fundamentally identity-based, predicated upon African American experience and identity, but it is largely not identity-exclusive. Over 140 years it has evolved through several distinct iterations, incorporating new concepts and serving the pressing needs of the community at each juncture.

Terminology (and Boundaries)

The question of whether Hebrew Israelites can or should be considered Jews is still hotly contested. In various publications, Isaac and Key have argued that they should be, and that the failure of the Jewish world to do so stems from racism. Isaac's challenge to the boundaries of Jewish identity is unlikely to be taken up by the Jewish community, and certainly not by the Orthodox.[5] However, it can and should inform the perspective of scholars. It is not the business of most scholars to accept or reject religious orthodoxy's categorizations. Within the Abrahamic traditions, many groups consider others to be outside of orthodox Christianity and Islam, even if their reasons are doctrinal rather than genealogical. In contrast, scholars must go by self-description and therefore, generally should respect how groups describe themselves, as Black Jews, Black Hebrews, or simply as Israelites, while acknowledging that the majority of the Jewish world do not accept this. Most studies have in fact done

---

[4] There is also the possibility of some Africans descending from Sephardic Jews who traveled southward after the Iberian expulsions of 1492 and 1497.

[5] Simply, we should understand that acceptance *as Jews* by Jewish religious authorities depends upon two criteria: *either* conversion or descent; and practice/knowledge. If descent cannot be proven, conversion is required. However, Isaac's argument is principally regarding how scholarship on Black Jews/Hebrew Israelites must be performed differently than on white Jews. Here, my response is that Isaac is largely correct, but some middle ground which acknowledges the prevalent attitudes of the Jewish establishment should be sought.

just this, terming the congregations "Black Jews." This created its own problems, as the positing of a "Black Judaism" implies that regular Judaism is white. I have chosen the term Black Hebrew Israelites for this text for a number of reasons, although it is no longer favored by the community in question. Those within the movement refer to themselves as Israelites, Hebrew Israelites, or, less commonly, Black Jews. In previous times, Black Hebrew Israelites and Black Jews were used often by members, but as their visibility has grown members have dropped the racial signifier, and it is now sometimes claimed that this is either offensive or redundant, as to be a Hebrew Israelite is already to be Black, while the term Jewish has become increasingly associated with the white Jewish community. On the other hand, the Southern Poverty Law Center (SPLC) recently decided to drop the "Black" from BHI due to growing Hispanic and Native American membership. For the wider world, belief in coterminous Black Israelite identity is not shared, and the additional signifier helps to clarify the subject matter. Indeed, Blackness is a crucial element of the movement – it is at its core. As Key writes, "The use of 'Black' . . . is to indicate that the Judaism being practiced by Hebrew Israelites is a denomination of Black Religion and not simply to differentiate it from 'white' Judaism. Black serves as an indicator that Black Judaism emerges out of the historical experiences of African Americans as 'blacks'" (Key 2011: 7–8). Additionally, even if many groups accept non-Black members, they still hold the axiomatic claim that the ancient Israelites *were* Black. Most popular reports still use BHI due to its familiarity.

Isaac argues that the Hebrew Israelite community must be seen as inextricably intertwined with the Black Jewish community because many members of the latter began as the former, and because many still straddle the divide.[6] Bruce Haynes (2018) confirms that such boundary crossing is quite common: not only is this the case between what he considers the "ideal types" of Black Jews and Hebrew Israelites, where many exist in the spectrum in between, but also within the Hebrew Israelite "denominations" themselves. We will cover many such individuals and congregations that emerge in one school before relocating to another. However, it should be recognized that certainly not all BHIs had any prior familial connection with Judaism – it is a small minority. Moreover, a number of Black Jews have been among the strongest critics of Hebrew Israelism. In the twenty-first century Black Jewish writer and activist Shais Rishon, who uses the pen name MaNishtana, has been a vocal opponent,

---

[6] A problem with this approach is that it does not recognize the degree to which many varieties of BHI, intentionally or otherwise, locate themselves clearly outside the boundary of Judaism, while applying that term to themselves. This is to say, they hold to beliefs and/or practices which they know prevent their acceptance by *any* other Jews as Jews (for example the worship of Christ). Simple self-definition, in such cases, can only take us so far.

arguing that since every sect of BHI has been founded by previously practicing Christians, this cannot be considered a Jewish movement, nor its members Jews (MaNishtana 2012). Black Jewish poet Tova Ricardo has opined that Hebrew Israelites are a vocal minority considered ridiculous by Black Jews, and she avers that the feeling is mutual. Hebrew Israelites, especially those of the more radical variety, very often dislike Black Jews (Podcast against Antisemitism, 2023). Even in the 1960s, prominent Black convert Robert Coleman publicly campaigned against the Hebrew Israelites, writing several opinion pieces for Jewish newspapers.

It is thus important for scholars not to risk conflating Black Jews and Black Hebrew Israelites simply because of their race. And certainly, BHI is unique; it should not be subsumed as one "denomination" of Judaism. Its history, ideology, and practice set it apart, as does the fluidity of movement between different groups. In addition, the enormous diversity of groups within BHI means that while some groups consider themselves Rabbinic Jews – simply ones not accepted by most of the rabbinic community – many others would balk at any association of themselves with white Jews, and reject any non-biblical literature.

My approach is to bear in mind that BHI may constitute a specifically Black interpretation of Judaism, in the same way that the Nation of Islam and the Black Church are specifically Black interpretations of Islam and Christianity. However, some iterations have been much closer in nature to (Black) Christianity or (Black) Islam, than to (white) Judaism. Therefore, we must understand the umbrella movement as one equidistant from all non-Black religions, while drawing upon them all, but with a specific form (Rabbinic BHI) which stands exactly at the boundary of Judaism. BHI takes an independently minded approach to the scriptures and traditions of those faiths, and through them foregrounds the priorities, narratives, history, and interests of Black Americans.

"Black Hebrew Israelism/Israelite[s]" thus offers a term which is immediately clear in its application. "Black Jew[s]" will be reserved for those individuals accepted as part of the rabbinic Jewish community, as will "white Jew[s]," when it is important to note their race. For the established Rabbinic Jewish world of Ashkenazi, Sephardi, Mizrachi, Ethiopian, and other forms of ethnic Jewry, I will risk controversy by referring to them simply as Jews and Judaism, with no racial signifier due to the universal racial mixture that is modern Judaism. It is hoped that all readers will remember that these terms therefore do not presume whiteness.

Black Hebrew Israelism is not limited to the United States. From the outset, groups and members have sought to spread the doctrine abroad, the Caribbean and Africa being the obvious first stopping points. There are now Hebrew Israelite groups in many countries, including the United Kingdom, France, and Germany. Except for one group that established itself in Israel, these extra-American congregations are not as significant as the American, and the evolution of the movement has taken place entirely within the United States. While these groups will be mentioned when relevant, other Black and Judaizing or emerging Jewish movements, such as those of the Lemba, Igbo, and so on in Africa, are not relevant to the discussion here. As with the Ethiopian Beta Israel, they are most often used by Hebrew Israelites at arm's length as constituting evidence for their claims but are otherwise separate from them. Judaizing communities have emerged all over the world during the course of the twentieth century, and most aim to adopt Rabbinic Judaism or mimic it as closely as they can (Bruder 2008; Lis et al. 2016). The Hebrew Israelites are unusual because they have taken their own direction. As will be argued here, the reason for this can largely be attributed to the evolution of the Black liberation struggle in the United States, which empowered Black Americans to create a form of Israelite identification with unique qualities, and/or stripped of any European elements.

Section Breakdown

The sections of this Element will follow the historical schema developed by Dorman (2013). This analysis illuminates how BHI has evolved through distinct iterations, at each stage drawing new impetus from the shifting environment of Black American life. He argued for three generations or waves, to which I add a fourth:

The first wave was a Judaized Christianity, which emerged from Holiness churches at the end of the nineteenth century, combining slave traditions with Masonic symbolism and several other sources to create racially mixed congregations. This wave consists of the Holiness quarter of Key's typology.

The second wave emerged in post-World War I New York, comprising the Rabbinic/Ethiopian Hebrew movement which was often led by Caribbean immigrants, and incorporating Garveyism, New Thought, and Millennialism. Most of these groups are rabbinic, but some display a movement toward Cultural Nationalism, and some later groups are Torah-only.

The next wave consisted of the Black Power generation, which grew up largely in and around Chicago. This was strongly Black nationalist, Afrocentric, literary, and influenced by the Nation of Islam. These groups can all be described as Cultural Nationalists, although some are Messianic and some are Torah-only.

Finally, I add a fourth wave that encompasses the new groups that have attracted the spotlight in the twenty-first century. These have emerged largely, again, from New York, mostly from the One West Camp, and are known as media-savvy and highly visible aggressive urban street preachers. These groups are Messianic Cultural Nationalists.

Almost every group has undergone some kind of schism, division, or propagation, leading to a dense network of related groups within and across waves. These will be tracked across sections.

Each of these sections examines pertinent topics, including the sources of BHI, issues of identity and conversion, state intervention and the use of violence by some BHI, and the question of BHI as a racial separatist movement.

1 First Wave: Nineteenth-Century Roots

There are two individuals acknowledged as the effective founders of BHI: William Christian and William S. Crowdy. They shared a great deal. They were both born enslaved, in the American South, were previously active in the Baptist church, and were committed Prince Hall Freemasons. They both established churches which quickly reached across the United States, and even outside it, and still exist today. Despite this, there are differences between them, and there is no record of the two meeting or acknowledging each other.

Baptist minister William Christian (1856–1928), though born in Mississippi, preached in Arkansas. He received a revelation in 1888 and in 1889 established the Church of the Living God (Christian Workers for Fellowship), teaching that the Israelites were Black and African Americans were their descendants. Sharing in the rapid expansion of Pentecostalism across the United States, by 1906, he had established 68 branches across the South and Midwest, which counted 4,276 members. At its peak in 1926, there were 239 churches and 17,402 members. Landing describes Christian's teachings as bearing three central themes: "the origins of the black race; Christian racial harmony; and select terminology reflecting some Ethiopianism and Masonic influence" (Landing 2002: 46).

William Saunders Crowdy (1847–1908), born in Maryland, worked as a cook and served as a Baptist deacon in Oklahoma for twenty-five years before receiving a series of visions in 1893. He began preaching across the Midwest, founding the first tabernacle of his Church of God and Saints of Christ (COGASOC) in Kansas in 1896. Like Christian's, his message spread quickly, since he traveled extensively, seeding new branches. COGASOC continued to grow after his death, and by 1936, it counted 213 tabernacles in 27 states with

37,084 members. Many small businesses were founded from within COGASOC.

Both Crowdy and Christian were fundamentally Christian in nature. Their rituals, their theology, their liturgy, and their terminology were all drawn from the Baptist Holiness tradition. Both emphasized repentance and worship of Christ. Both were temperance advocates, and Christian even prohibited smoking cigars. Christian and Crowdy shared a message of antiracist unity, their churches being home to mixed congregations of Black and white members during the time of Jim Crow legislation. They held that not only African Americans but Native Americans and Asians were also lost Israelite tribes. While both taught the importance of following the Ten Commandments, Crowdy was also interested in restoring some practices of the Old Testament. By 1906 members of the COGASOC were following the Jewish calendar and feast days, observing shabbat on Saturday, and using some Hebrew. From this beginning, his church grew progressively more Judaic in its practices after his death. However, neither of these leaders had any contact with living Jews, deriving their practices from the Old Testament.

Crowdy's missionaries established a branch in South Africa in 1903, and in Jamaica in 1920, making COGASOC the first pan-African iteration of BHI. Another COGASOC congregation in Rusape, Zimbabwe, has progressed in a rabbinic direction – although not converted, they follow the norms of Rabbinic Judaism, relying on Zimbabwe's Jewish community to help them with books, and believe themselves to descend from a lost Israelite tribe.

Seven years after receiving his revelation, Christian published a book: *Poor Pilgrim's Work, in the Name of Father, Son and Holy Ghost on Christian Friendship Works* (1896). The preface opens with the statement, "Free Mason religion is the true mode of all religion. All other modes of religion are not worth one cent." (1896: i) Christian goes on to assert a distinct racial binary. Drawing a straight line from Adam to Christ, all of whom were Black, he identifies Blacks as "black Jew[s]" or "Etheopean[s]" [sic] (1896: 4). He explains his certainty in the Blackness of the Israelites with several scriptural references: "I am become like a bottle in the smoke" (Ps.119:83); "My skin is black upon me" (Job 30:30); "I am black" (Jer. 8:21), and "I am black but comely" (Song of Songs 1:5) (1896: 5–6). This is in contrast to the gentiles, who descend from the Fallen Angels and "are now called Caucasians or white people" (1896: 4). This collapsing of the Jewish–gentile binary into the racial typology of the United States will be found throughout BHI. Christian, however, in offering a non-Adamic source for whites/gentiles, inverted the racial order promoted by many racists of the time (Parfitt 2020). While whites presumed their own descent from Adam and puzzled over the origin of Blacks, Christian made a scriptural argument for the Blackness of Adam and the Israelites, leaving whites to be sired from corrupt spiritual beings. (We should also recognize this as predicting the Nation of Islam [NOI] teaching that whites are devils, Dorman 2013). Other than this, and a strongly stated opposition to racism, the text is indiscernible from any work of Christian ministry.

Like Christian, Crowdy also published a text – *The Revelation of God Revealed* (1902) – and it too is difficult to discern much outside of contemporaneous restorationist Protestantism within it, although Crowdy's bears no mention of race whatsoever. This text is written largely as questions, with directions to a biblical verse provided as answers. One crucial feature of Crowdy's text is his exhortation to keep the sabbath on the seventh day (Saturday), although even this is argued fundamentally from New Testament citations. Even when discussing the commandments of Moses, he limits these strictly to the Ten Commandments, and, indeed, he rejects circumcision as being no longer relevant, based upon the sayings of Paul. Furthermore, he argues that the Torah's dietary restrictions should not be taken seriously, similarly based on New Testament citations. Christian meanwhile states that Saturday is the sabbath, but does not keep it himself because, "I can't find where Jesus told me to keep it; moreover, Jesus Christ himself, healed on the Sabbath day" (Christian 1896: 33). Therefore, "don't ask me, do I keep the Sabbath day, but ask me, do I keep the words of our Lord and Savior Jesus Christ" (1896: 34). It is difficult to imagine a more Christian response.

The third figure we can include in this wave is Frank S. Cherry (c.1868–1963), about whom less is known. He claimed to have founded his Church of the Living God, the Pillar Ground of Truth for All Nations in Chattanooga, Tennessee in 1886, although there are no independent records of this. The church appears first in Philadelphia in 1915. It seems likely that Cherry was influenced by Crowdy, though he never admitted this and his church was always distinctly independent. Both the beliefs and the sartorial style of Cherry and his followers mimic those of Crowdy's COGASOC, yet they deny that any other Black Jews existed (Dorman 2013). Crowdy lived in and ran COGASOC from Philadelphia from 1899 until 1903; and the headquarters remained there, maintained by the Crowdy–Plummer faction after his death until 1917, when they relocated to Virginia, so many would have heard him preach there.

The most important report on Cherry (Fauset 1944) is late, far from comprehensive, and contains several apparent errors. However, it appears that Cherry was more idiosyncratic than Christian and Crowdy, advocating several doctrines which would later take hold among more radical Hebrew Israelites. He taught that Blacks were the original humans and Jews, and utilized Rev. 2:9 and 3:9's description of "a synagogue of Satan" who "say that they are Jews, but are not," to argue that Rabbinic Jews were "an interloper and a fraud" – probably the first BHI example of this now-famous usage. He sourced the origin of whiteness in the leprosy placed upon Gehazi the Amalekite (2 Kings 5:27). Like Christian and Crowdy, he believed in Jesus as savior, but unlike them, he taught that slavery was the result of the Israelites' disobedience – a doctrine which would become universal among BHIs. He held a developed eschatology which predicted the year 2000 as the end of the Gentile Age (the third 2,000-year period of creation), and the beginning of the seventh millennium, the sabbath era.[7] This new age would see the world destroyed in an Arab-Israeli war, and the true (Black) Israelites returned to their renewed homeland. The only afterlife he foresaw is the resurrection, wherein righteous saints will be reconstituted before the wicked are destroyed forever. Until then, they were to follow the Ten Commandments to ensure their safe transition (Fauset 2001; Rubel 2009).

Gambling, smoking, swearing, and, eventually, television and movies were forbidden by Cherry, although moderate alcohol usage was encouraged, based on biblical precedent. The leaders however were permitted to swear. After Prophet Cherry's death, he was succeeded by his son "Prince" Benjamin F. Cherry.

The churches established by these three pioneers persist to this day. Cherry's single church still exists at 2132 Nicholas Street, Philadelphia, although his influence belies that single establishment. Christian's Church of the Living God has shrunk but is still present as a basically Pentecostal denomination, with membership estimated at around 40,000.[8] Crowdy's COGASOC remains probably the largest BHI congregation, although it split into several factions after his death. The major two were led by his first ordained Bishop, the white James Grove, and his own nephew, Joseph Crowdy. There currently exist at least five distinct organizations claiming linear descent from his establishment. The COGASOC (descending from Grove's faction)[9] and Temple Beth El (from the Crowdy line)[10] are the largest and most obvious, the latter having branches in several African states as well as Cuba and Jamaica. The former is obviously Christian in orientation, but the latter has progressively Judaized. This was largely the work of Howard Z. Plummer, leader from the early 1960s until 1975. He was the first to take the title Rabbi and argued that while Crowdy had made the first steps, their journey should progressively bring them closer to the religion of the Torah and

---

[7] This tripartite 7,000 year structure, culminating in both the ascent of Africans and the return of the Jews, is evidenced previously in the nineteenth-century Black theologians J. T. Holly and T. G. Steward (Fulop 1991).

[8] www.ctlgcwff.com.   [9] www.cogsoconline.org/.   [10] www.cogasoc.org/.

the prophets. Their website states, "Judaism provides a complete guide for relegating all aspects of human life to the will of God. (Judaism is for us neither a race nor a culture, but it is a manner of believing, a tried and true means through which love of, and faith in God is channelled into upright living.)"[11] Despite this, much of the Mosaic Law is not followed strictly, the dietary laws being perceived as cultural beliefs absorbed from Mesopotamia, and not relevant today (Srole 1978). Jesus is understood to be a prophet, and the New Testament is considered an organic part of scripture. According to Rubel, "The Christ Spirit is 'simply the anointed power of God.' According to Church teaching, prophet Crowdy was a Christ, as were all of his successors" (Rubel 2009: 58)

In fact, these groups are best described as advocating "Judaism as it *should* be practiced" (Srole 1978: 13, my emphasis). Even for those groups such as Temple Beth El, that believe that there is a progression from Judaic Christianity into Judaism, the Judaism they imagine reaching is not the Judaism of Ashkenazi or Sephardic Jews; it is reconstructed biblical Judaism. Thus, although they accept some trappings of Rabbinic Judaism, they do not accept any of the innovations in doctrine or practice made by rabbis. One member interviewed by Srole says,

> Our doctrine comes from God through His prophets. The Bible says in Amos 3:7, "Surely the Lord God shall do nothing but He revealeth His secrets unto His servant the prophet." Now, to find God's secrets you have to search through His prophets. We don't follow man's teaching. We don't follow any angel. But we follow God through His prophets. We find out what God wants, us to do, what He's revealing to us. Our emphasis is not on post-Biblical tradition but on the Scripture itself that has the authority of Biblical support. (Srole 1978: 13)

This quote indicates an important point that remains true of many BHI groups: their reliance upon the Bible is absolute, and it is believed that the Bible can be read independently of any tradition of interpretation, because if the reader is genuine, God speaks to them through it.

There are many other congregations similar to those described here. These include the New Covenant Congregation of Israel (NCCI), founded in Georgia in 1975 by Yachov Ben Yisrael. The NCCI refuses the designator Hebrew Israelite, but has much the same doctrines and practices as Temple Beth El – indeed their congregation in North Carolina is also called Temple Beth El. Another, Israel of God, based in Chicago with congregations in other states, identifies as Christian, adhering to the Christian covenant while upholding

---

[11] www.cogasoc.org/about/this-we-believe-2/.

many Jewish practices such as dietary regulations.[12] While teaching that Christ is divine, the latter rejects the Holy Spirit. Many such groups are indistinguishable from those within the Messianic Jewish, Sacred Name, Worldwide Church of God, and Hebrew Roots movements, except for their belief in the Blackness of the Israelites.

One post-Crowdy organization that has consistently been overlooked is the Independent Church of God and Saints of Christ (ICOGASOC). Established by one of Crowdy's most favored supporters, its founder is one of the very few women to have created a BHI congregation.

Born in Virginia, Malinda Morris (nee Carter, 1867–1937) was an early follower of Crowdy, who was selected to found a tabernacle in Newark. She soon gained enough followers to rent a storefront and then to build a church. She became a local celebrity who traveled by horse and carriage, then by luxury cars, and managed several businesses: a grocery, restaurant, butcher, and day nursery, as well as summer youth programs, and a shelter for widows, orphans, and fire victims. She was so highly regarded by the COGASOC membership as to acquire the title Queen, and some members even wore a pin with her likeness on it, next to Crowdy's.

After Crowdy's death – at Morris's home, where he had been visiting – the two factions began to pull COGASOC apart, and Morris withdrew from the legal war that was beginning. She believed that her own leadership was prophesied, and her ICOGASOC was incorporated on December 24, 1909 (Miller 2023b). The ICOGASOC itself still exists on Jones Street in Newark, and is to all intents and purposes a Christian church. In 2014, a section of Jones Street was renamed in honor of Morris – Queen Melinda Dora Morris Way.

One member of Morris's ICOGASOC further strove out on his own. Bishop Allan Wilson Cook (aka Rabbi Haling Hank Lenht, 1872–1935) was ordained by Morris and was loyal to her, but founded his own variation of the church which took the theology in a new and prescient direction. Born in Virginia, Cook was the free-born son of a slave and a mixed race, Black Jewish woman. (It is unclear whether his mother was Black and white Jewish, or Black Jewish and white). He had a religious experience at age eleven, which provided the message he would bring to the world. He moved to Montclair, New Jersey where he worked and studied for some years, marrying in 1890. Cook was selected to lead an ICOGASOC congregation in Montclair in 1910. In 1913, he relocated to Yonkers, New York, where he founded his own Independent Church of God of the Juda Tribe of Israel. While the church was incorporated as a place of worship in Yonkers, by 1925, it had moved to the much more

---

[12] https://theisraelofgod.com; Malone 2017: 17–18.

popular Harlem. It was in 1925 that Cook published a short booklet, in which he set out his biography, his religious thought, his conception of America's race problem, and his devotion to Marcus Garvey. Cook was a thinker ahead of his time in several ways, and in his text, we can see the beginnings of a transition from the Pentecostal emphasis of the first generation of BHIs, to a more rigorous, and more Jewish, position which characterizes the second generation (Miller 2023b).

First, Cook demonstrates already a movement toward a stronger assertion of Jewish identity, if not practice, which sets him apart from his forerunners. Having removed reference to Christ from the church name, Cook replaced it with a direct reference to the Tribe of Juda. The keeping of the commandments was the key responsibility and path to redemption, rather than imitating Christ.

Second, unlike Crowdy and Christian, who operated intentionally color-blind churches, Cook took race consciousness a step further. His church is clearly aimed at Blacks, who have a special destiny and a particular responsibility. Cook asserted an ongoing Black Jewish identity, where the two terms are synonymous: Jews are Black and Blacks are Jews. Cook accepted the white Jewish community (one of the Church's seven trustees was a Russian Jewish pharmacist, David Rudy), but held them to be descended from the Lost Tribes, who intermarried with Persians, thus lightening their complexion.

Third, Cook provides the first recorded use of Deuteronomy 28 (see below) as a proof text for his claim that African Americans are the Children of Israel.

A final overlooked group that originated in Crowdy's COGASOC can mark the end of this section: a musical group called the Flamingos. This doo-wop four-piece band was formed in 1952 in Chicago by two sets of cousins: Ezekiel (1933–1999) and Jake (1926–1997) Carey – both born in Virginia – and Paul Wilson (1935–1988) and Johnny Carter (1934–2009) – both born in Chicago. All four were members of the COGASOC and described themselves as Black Jews or Black Hebrews. According to a report in a Cleveland, Ohio, newspaper, they turned down lucrative bookings due to their observance of Jewish holidays and shabbat, and were major contributors to a Temple in Belleville, Virginia. They achieved notable success through the 1950s and 1960s, being inducted into the Rock and Roll Hall of Fame in 2001, and the Doo-Wop Hall of Fame in 2004 (Young 1961; Baptista 2019).

Textual Sources

The earliest exponents of Black Israelism were all born Christian, and, with the exception of Cook, maintained their faith in Christ as the Messiah. Both of these features would diminish throughout the subsequent stages, as new generations began to be born into the culture of Hebrew Israelism. Scholars have usually understood this first stage of BHI practice to be Judaic Christianity: it is considered as an outgrowth of the existing Christianity of former enslaved persons, and of the emerging Black Church establishment. In attempting to go *back* to Judaism, these groups are really trying to recreate an earlier, more Judaic, and thus more *authentic* version of Christianity. That is, a religion which looks like that found in the apostolic church of the New Testament. Landing describes it as "a black Christian response to black life, a black message from black leaders to black people; and an appeal to both blacks and whites in a society with deep racial divisions" (Landing 2002: 69).

Most scholars presume that a crucial part of the heritage of BHI was a fascination with the tribulation of the Israelites under the various empires that dominated them, and in particular with the bondage in Egypt and Babylon. Albert Raboteau describes how, "Exodus became dramatically real, especially in the songs and prayer meetings of the slaves who reenacted the story as they shuffled in the ring dance they called the "Shout." In the ecstasy of worship, time and distance collapsed, and the slaves *became* the Children of Israel" (Raboteau 1995: 33–4; italics in original). In a ritual form well known to scholars of religion, identification with the mythical hero is achieved through the symbolic replication of their quest; in repeating their actions, and undergo-ing the dangers as they did, the neophyte temporarily becomes the hero. Stepping into mythical time, ontological difference collapses and archetypal actions create an intimate connection between the current performer and the protagonist of the legend (Eliade 1959). This participation is a kind of real-ization, whereby the eternal is manifested in the temporal, nourishing it and giving it life. By creating the connection with the archetypal experience of Israel, enslaved Africans were attempting to bring into their future the same divine assistance that saved Israel. We will see that the most radical Hebrew Israelite groups that are heir to this tradition have continued to evoke mythical time, identifying themselves with biblical heroes and bringing the narrative of the Bible to bear on the present, perceiving the mythical in the phenomenal. And arguably, just as the Egyptian bondage which formed the Israelites into a people, whereupon the mixed multitude would receive the direct revelation from God, of the Torah, so too the multitude of African peoples enslaved in America became one – African Americans – through that process. Here then, we have a re-enacting of the myth of origins, rather than creation. We might speculate that the invocations of sacred time and the myth of the Exodus have served, now, to create a new Children of Israel, one whose Exodus is still ongoing.

Perhaps eclipsing even Exodus in significance for BHIs, is Deuteronomy 28. This chapter, containing a long list of curses and miseries that the Israelites would endure should they not follow the commandments that God has laid down, became the single most important biblical passage for the Hebrew Israelite movement, being routinely provided as the best piece of evidence for the claim of Israelite descent. Specific citations often focus on prophecies that Israelites will be taken as slaves to Egypt on boats (Deut. 28:68). Egypt is here interpreted metaphorically as designating the new enslavement in America. The predicted tribulations of the Israelites are thought to describe the condition of Africans in America.

The first recorded use of this passage was by Cook. Prior to this, those trying to justify their argument could make only dubious references to biblical passages wherein an Israelite seems to assert darkness of skin, such as those given by William Christian. These references are untenable given their contexts, where they are clearly metaphorical expressions of despair (with the exception of Song of Songs 1:5, in which the speaker is not King Solomon but a woman). These facts are inescapable when read in the original Hebrew, and some are only apparitions of the King James translation. Cook's use of Deuteronomy 28 presented not only the introduction of a new passage of scripture but also a new method of proof. While previous thinkers sought evidence that the Israelites were Black and then assumed a continuity through the American Black population, Deuteronomy 28 presents a prophecy which is putatively fulfilled by Black America, thereby making a direct connection between the Bible and present circumstances. Many of the One West groups we will meet in the final section argue that this scriptural proof overcomes any nonscriptural arguments or evidence against their claims, as well as disproving Jewish claims to Israelite heritage. Deuteronomy 28 now constitutes the central piece of Hebrew Israelite scripture and polemic; this is the passage cited most often as proof of identity claims, and which has reputedly had a striking impact on some listeners. The potency of this passage depends upon its capacity to both explain Black suffering in America, and to subtly suggest a solution. It is only when the Israelites return to God and take up again the commandments that the curse shall be lifted, and their suffering will end. The chapter then acts as both an intellectual and emotional motivation for accepting these claims and adopting Hebrew Israelite practice.

Deuteronomy 28 is usually combined with Genesis 15:13, which predicts a 400-year period of slavery for Abraham's descendants. The Israelites' time in Egypt does not equal 400 years, whereas it can be argued that African American bondage has now been more than 400 years.

A third oft-cited passage is Ezekiel's vision of the Valley of the Dry Bones (Ezek. 37). This metaphor for communal redemption and revivification from a place of absolute despair, has long been used by Black Americans to signify their hope for their own redemption. For BHIs, however, Ezekiel's vision becomes a direct prophecy about their condition, namely their social death and their resurrection from it.

It is striking that, for Hebrew Israelites, the Bible is not simply a book of history. Everything said by the prophets is made to fit the last 400 years of American history. As such, the entire Bible is transplanted into the present, with seamless relevance. Like many religions emerging from oppressed groups, BHI presents an opportunity to gain reprieve from a harsh reality by providing a mythical superstructure which makes suffering and struggle meaningful. It directly counteracts the imposed low esteem of Black America by making Black Americans God's chosen people. It interprets America as a ruthlessly unequal society where the oppressed are burdened by poverty, poor health, low employment, and lack of agency; an evil kingdom from which the righteous are struggling to return to God and break the subtle but potent psychological bonds which oppressors have imposed. The imminence of apocalyptic expectation in many groups indicates the desire and the necessity of radical change, and even an inversion of the oppressed–oppressor vector (see Section 4).

A more recent reference is Joseph Williams' *Hebrewisms of West Africa* (1930). This text aimed to demonstrate and explain the similarities between Israelite and some African cultures, including marriage practices, separation of women from men during menstruation, and linguistic forms. Williams explained this by a migration of Judeans (though no other Israelites) through Africa. The book has been cited repeatedly since its publication and forms a mainstay of Hebrew Israelite evidence. There is a certain amount of misreading or cherry-picking in many of these cases, since Williams is certain that Jews also descend from Israelites, and that the Israelites were not Black in the modern sense, but the significance of a text by a white scholar supporting BHI claims cannot be dismissed.

Despite the heavy reliance of BHI on Jewish and Christian scripture, we should also not minimize the fact that all of the first generation of Hebrew Israelites were Freemasons. This has been established for Christian, Crowdy, and Cherry; Morris was an active member of the Order of the Eastern Star and Cook seems likely to have been a Mason though there is yet no definitive proof. Dorman (2013) has argued that the influence of Masonic concepts regarding the significance of the Israelites, and especially those parts absorbed/shared by British Israelism, was critical to the first generation. The role of Prince Hall Masonry in African American religion, particularly in the early twentieth century, is still little understood and deserves more focused research.

2 Second Wave: 1920s Harlem

This section will explore the "Rabbinic" or "Ethiopian Hebrew" variant of Hebrew Israelism, which developed in 1920s Harlem and still maintains a strong presence there. This version was created by the influx of Caribbean immigrants into the United States – and particularly into New York – during the early years of the twentieth century. Ever since scholars began investigating Harlem's Black Jews they have suggested that the large, usually Sephardic, Jewish presence in the Caribbean since the sixteenth century may be implicated.

A core part of the attraction of Hebrew Israelite thought is surely the assertion of a strong and historical national identity for American Blacks. The idea that African Americans are and always have been *a people,* with all that goes along with that – a homeland, a shared history, a place in the global organization of peoples distinct from that of white America – can instill a sense of pride naturally lacking in a people whose original identity has been suppressed for centuries. The capacity to meaningfully distinguish the peoplehood of Black America from that of white America is certainly important. This was articulated in several ways during the twentieth century, including by the Moorish Science Temple (MST). Founded in 1913 by Noble Drew Ali (Timothy Drew), the MST claimed that Blacks were really Moors and therefore should reject the term Negro as an offensive appellation created by whites. In the NOI, this became an assertion of descent from the tribe of Shabazz and of Muslim identity more generally. Both of these groups, like BHI, explicitly shunned the term Negro in favor of self-chosen designations.

Surpassing the influence of Moorish identity claims, was that of Ethiopia, which had a greater attractive force for many. Ethiopia was the sole African nation to never have been successfully conquered by European powers, maintaining its independence throughout the modern period. The Greek term Ethiopia, meaning burnt/dark-faced is ancient, and in antiquity was frequently used for the whole of Africa. Thus, all Africans could claim to be Ethiopian. Ethiopia is mentioned in the Bible, indicating its long and impressive history; and it adopted Christianity long before European nations. While Ethiopianism, as an early iteration of Afrocentrism, was a passing trend, the well-publicized discovery of the Ethiopian Beta Israel (or Falasha) community of Black Jews in the nineteenth century inspired several early BHI congregations to name themselves as EHCs. By aligning themselves with a known community of Black Jews they were able to appear more legitimate, and several leaders asserted their own Ethiopian descent, although this has (almost) always proved fallacious (Parfitt and Semi 2002).

Born in Barbados, Arnold Josiah Ford (1877–1935) immigrated to Harlem in 1911. Ford was an important figure for Harlem's BHI movement, being especially interested in forging a more rabbinic direction. It is said that he learned everything he knew of Hebrew and Judaism from white Jews in America. Indeed, it was only upon observing white Jews in Harlem that he recognized his own parents' habits as crypto-Jewish.[13] He cofounded the Moorish Zionist Temple (MZT) in 1921, with two individuals who shared his interest in Freemasonry, Judaism, and Garveyism: Samuel Valentine and Mordecai Herman.[14] It was clearly influenced by Drew Ali's MST, although MZT (and its school, the Moorish Palestine Talmud Torah) was intentionally multiracial. The cooperation did not last long, however, and Ford and Valentine left to form Beth B'nai Abraham (BBA) in 1923.[15] It was the BBA that introduced many rabbinic elements to Hebrew Israelism; however, Ford's was "a polycultural religion that drew from many sources – including aspects of Judaism, Freemasonry, Garveyism, Theosophy, Christianity, and Islam" (Dorman 2013: 130). Ford was committed to the race, and the adoption of Judaism may have been only a part of a much broader vision of renewal and uplift. He claimed that Black Americans were "the Ethiopian Falasha and [hence] the Biblical Hebrews," and unsuccessfully petitioned for the adoption of Judaism as the official religion of the Universal Negro Improvement Association (UNIA). Ford emigrated to Ethiopia in 1930 with a few of his followers. Following Ford's departure, Rabbi Israel ben Yamin (or ben Newman/Nooman, founder of Congregation Beth Zion) was ordained at MZT in 1929, and it was subsequently led by the blind Rabbi Hezekiah Jacob (born Steven Lee, d.1940). Jacob preached the unity of Black and white Jews, and while the majority of the congregation were West Indian and Native American, some 20 percent were white.

More famous than Ford is his student/rival, Wentworth Arthur Matthew (1892–1973). Surely the most important figure in the history of Hebrew Israelism, Matthew claimed to have been born in a Falasha village in Lagos, Nigeria, where his grandfather was a Falasha cantor. Multiple problems disprove this account: there is no record of Ethiopian Jews in Nigeria, the

---

[13] Ford was baptized, and during his time in the British Navy his religion was recorded as Church of England. Dorman notes, "His remembrances of secret familial traditions passed down through his mother could reflect a range of prior traditions, which could bear resemblance to Hebraic ones, from Jewish traditions passed down from an Ashkenazi or Sephardic ancestor in the Caribbean, to African folkways, or to the Sabbath-keeping and dietary regulations of Seventh Day Adventism" (Dorman 2013: 129).

[14] Herman has been immortalized in Jerusalem by Israeli street artist Solomon Souza (Kestenbaum 2016).

[15] Valentine, a Jamaican by birth, later left the BBA to lead a congregation more aligned with European Judaism. His children attended Yeshiva.

Ethiopian Jews have no such position as cantor, and he is known to have been born on the Caribbean island of St. Kitts. That he was of Christian background is demonstrated by the fact that the first iteration of his congregation, Commandment Keepers, Church of the Living God, Pillar and Ground of the Truth, established in 1919, was Protestant in orientation. The church progressively Judaized, but its worship retained Christian ritual elements, iconography, and hymns even in 1929. It appears to have been from Ford's influence that Matthew adopted the "Ethiopian Hebrew" terminology in the title of his Masonic affiliate to the Commandment Keepers, the Royal Order of Ethiopian Hebrews, established in 1926. It was only after his rabbinic ordination that Matthew exchanged the title Bishop for Rabbi. The ordination certificate was proudly displayed in his office, signed by "Ethiopia's Chief Rabbi." (The document was indeed mailed from Ethiopia, but the signature is Arnold Ford's; the Beta Israel religious leader is not a rabbi but a *qes*). According to Brotz (1964), Matthew and his congregation realized that they were Falasha Ethiopian Hebrews only after learning of their coreligionists there. However, when Ethiopian Jewish intellectual Taamrat Emmanuel visited the United States in 1931, he attended their service, assured them that he was one with them, and they remained on friendly terms (Semi 2016).

Matthew did, however, have something of a command of Hebrew. This and the Jewish ritual elements gradually incorporated into the Commandment Keepers (CK) likely came from Jewish Harlemites, who either believed in the congregation's sincerity, or simply appreciated whatever remuneration was made.

Wentworth Matthew's theology, from what we can learn of it, seems to be a blend of different sources. He was a Freemason and incorporated some of the then-fashionable mysticism. He claimed that his Judaism contained a "Cabalistic element" which demonstrated its validity, although the cabalistic seals in his notes are copied (errors and all) from a nineteenth-century occult work. Matthew also adopted some of the motifs of New Thought from his Harlem peers. Dorman writes that "this 'Living God' philosophy . . . was one of the major influences on Rabbi Matthew's theology" (Dorman 2004: 184). He even claimed that he could tell an individual which tribe of Israel they descended from, by inspection of their physical features.

The Harlem explosion of what was called Black Judaism at the time was noticed and discussed throughout the 1920s. Although some white Jews attended the Commandment Keepers and MZT, the Jewish world more often judged these congregations to be simply fake Jews or Judaizers. It was only in the 1940s that Matthew's passionate denunciations of Jewish suffering under the Nazis' yoke turned the tide and, while still not fully accepting them as Jews, the Jewish world began to open its doors to Matthew. He spoke throughout the decade at synagogues, beginning a profitable venture as a guest speaker which would provide for his community through the lean times. It is perhaps due to this lowering of barriers that the 1940s, 1950s, and 1960s saw a growing promotion and acceptance of Jewish norms in ritual and practice in the New York groups.

Of at least eight BHI congregations in 1920s Harlem, the Commandment Keepers was the only one to survive the Depression. By 1947 it had three branches – Harlem, Brooklyn, and Youngstown, Ohio – with a total of possibly 200 members, although there were also three schismatic offshoots in Harlem, which counted 80 members between them. In 1949, they were able to purchase their main building, aided by a benefit concert organized by a Jewish philanthropist (Dorman 2012).

At the suggestion of Irving Block,[16] Matthew applied for membership on the New York Board of Rabbis in 1952, but his application was ultimately turned down – an experience which left him embittered. He was willing to be accepted only on terms of absolute equality, and under no circumstances was he willing to convert or accept a subordinate position for his community and traditions – an attitude which would become foundational for many of the groups stemming from the Commandment Keepers. Matthew did not want to become a Jew, indeed he insisted on maintaining his position that the Black Israelites were the original, both phenotypically and in terms of their tradition. The white Jews, he insisted, had mingled with gentiles, absorbing not just their looks but their ways.

Wentworth Matthew continued his attempts to court the Jewish community through the 1960s. He contacted Isaac Trainin of the Federation of Jewish Philanthropies, which led to the creation of a task force on Black Jews. The task force, and its success, were still limited, however, because without a fundamental change in the Jewish approach to *halakhah* (Rabbinic Jewish law), all that they, or any part of the Orthodox establishment, could offer was a pathway to conversion – exactly what Matthew and other Black Israelites perceived as offensive. However, the Federation did manage to secure places at Yeshivas and Jewish summer camps for the children, on the basis that they may decide to convert at the point of bar mitzvah (Dorman 2012).

After this rebuff, Matthew ceased seeking official acceptance from the Jewish community. Nevertheless, his active speaking schedule at Jewish institutions throughout the 1960s indicates his interest in reaching out to the normative Jewish world, and his hope that education would help his own people to be accepted. It was only in 2022 that the New York Board of Rabbis would

---

[16] Irving Block (1923–2002) was a decisively ecumenical Reform rabbi and long-time proponent of the Hebrew Israelites, along with his colleague Eliezer Brooks, who believed that many Caribbean Blacks descended from Sephardic Marranos intermarrying with their slaves.

recognize the Rabbinic BHI, when Capers Funnye and Baruch Yehudah were accepted as rabbis.

Rabbi Wentworth Arthur Matthew's legacy is long and indelible. He founded the first Black synagogue in the United States, taught and ordained dozens of rabbis, and created the basis for the spread of Rabbinic Hebrew Israelite Judaism around the nation. His contact with the Jewish world and his love of Jewish tradition have informed many of the leaders who followed him. Now in the third generation, the Rabbinic form of BHI has established itself as an important configuration in the United States.

The initial Commandment Keepers, however, would ultimately split acrimoniously after Matthew's death. By the 1980s, it had fallen into warring factions, led by his grandson David Dore (b. 1955) and his student Chaim White (d. 1997) (Ben Levy n.d.a). By the 2000s, the rift was so deep that the aging associates of the latter, who had de facto taken over the synagogue building, sold the property without informing their congregants so as not to see it fall into their enemies' hands.[17] Many of Matthew's students have gone on to create important congregations, however. A few can be listed here.

Yirmeyahu Yisrael (b. Julius Wilkins, 1912–1989) was ordained in 1940 and founded B'nai Adath Kol Beth Yisroel in 1954, in Brooklyn, with a greater emphasis on Jewish tradition.[18] The congregation grew quickly and in the mid-1960s purchased an old synagogue building which seated several hundred worshippers (Ben Levy n.d.b.). In 1964, however, a split occurred when a group, led by Cohen Levi Yisrael (b. Irvin Steward Wanzer, 1927–2014) and Moreh Yosayf, asserted that Black Jews should rethink *halakhah* in order to accord more with the Torah, rather than seeking to emulate white Jews.

Favoring an Afrocentric Torah-only approach, Yisrael and Yosayf formed Hashabah Yisrael in 1965, in Brooklyn. In addition to abandoning the Talmud, they took titles such as Cohen and Moreh rather than Rabbi, and sanctioned polygamy – Levi himself would take five wives in total. The two also adopted Afrocentric dress and drumming. Hashabah has two spin-off congregations. In 1978, Levi's student Cohane Michael ben Levi (b. James Young) moved to Guyana with two dozen followers who would become known as the Hebrew Family of Guyana (ben Levi would later throw his allegiance behind Ben Ammi's African Hebrew Israelites of Jerusalem [AHIJ], as described in his important *Israelites and Jews – The Significant Difference*). Levi's son Cohen

---

[17] Supporters of Dore maintain the website www.commandmentpillar.com. Dore was the second African American to graduate from Yeshiva University, having studied at YU High School before earning his Diploma in Hebraic Studies and B.A. from YU in 1977.

[18] https://bakby.org.

Shetmeyah Levi founded a congregation in Charlotte, North Carolina.[19] By 2008, the relocation of many members, and difficulties with the new building, led to the absorption of Levi's congregation into B'nai Adath, whose new leader, R. Baruch Yehudah, was able to create a workable balance of concepts and traditions (Ben Levy n.d.c.).

Rabbi Levi Ben Levy (b. Lawrence McKethan, Linden, North Carolina, 1935–1999) was introduced to the faith at age twenty-two when a coworker invited him to attend a Commandment Keepers service. He was instrumental in recreating Matthew's defunct rabbinical school in 1971 as the Israelite Rabbinical Academy, as well as creating the Israelite Board of Rabbis.[20] Matthew was made Chief Rabbi until his death, when Levy became the second Chief Rabbi (Ben Levy n.d.d.). Rabbi Sholomo Ben Levy is his son.

A more roundabout path was pursued by Avihu Reuben (b. Henry Brown, 1902–1991), who helped bring Matthew's teachings to Chicago. Born in Jackson, Tennessee, Reuben moved to Chicago in 1919 before adopting Judaism in 1925, apparently as a reaction to Christian racism. He is known to have worked closely with David Lazarus,[21] who was a fellow member of Marcus Garvey's UNIA. Together Reuben and Lazarus founded the True Ethiopian Foundation in the 1930s. The congregation would be restyled as the Congregation of Ethiopian Hebrews (CEH) sometime later. In the late 1940s, Reuben studied with Wentworth Matthew in New York, who ordained him as a rabbi, before he returned to Chicago in 1951. Matthew visited once every month for the next year to oversee their practice. The CEH, with its attached Ethiopian Hebrew Culture Center, was helped both financially and materially by the white Jewish community of Chicago. CEH counted 35 families in the mid-1960s, most of whom were originally from the Northeast United States. Also involved were instructors Lewis (or Louis) Green and Naphtali Israel. The CEH later merged with another congregation (Rosenzweig 1963; Landing 2002).

Hailu Moshe Paris (1933–2014) had a similarly complex but, if anything, more fascinating story. Paris had been born in Ethiopia, according to some sources to a family of Beta Israel (although he denied that this was certain), but was adopted by Eudora Paris, a member of BBA who had emigrated to Ethiopia with Ford. Upon the Italian invasion of Ethiopia in 1936 Eudora, Hailu, and Eudora's mother fled, along with a Torah scroll that Ford had brought from America. According to Hailu the boat they were on was searched for Jews by Nazis when it stopped in Germany, but their color saved them from suspicion.

---

[19] www.hashabahyisrael.org.   [20] www.blackjews.org/.
[21] Landing claims there were two Joseph Lazaruses, one the father of the other. It is unclear whether there were two or only one, and, if two, which one was Edward Witty, aka David Lazarus.

Arriving in New York, Hailu was then raised within Yirmeyahu and Ellis Mcleod's Kohol Beth B'nai Yisrael.[22] Demonstrating his broad background, he studied at Yeshiva University (where he won a scholarship to study Talmud and Jewish Studies in Israel for one year) and was a vocal advocate of African Jews of all kinds. His rabbinic training came from Matthew, however, and Paris served as an associate rabbi at Mount Horeb Congregation.[23] Hailu Paris was thus the one Harlem Hebrew Israelite who could legitimately claim Ethiopian – and perhaps Beta Israel – heritage. He was respected by the Jewish community and spoke at synagogues and Jewish organizations throughout the 1960s and 1970s. He also taught at Irving Block's Brotherhood Synagogue.

Other individuals found their way into Rabbinic BHI, independent of Rabbi Matthew. Abel Respes (1919–1986), for example, was born in Philadelphia and raised by parents who read the Bible and told him that they were Jews. At age twelve he was struck by lightning but survived, and had a religious experience when he was twenty-eight which convinced him to research his roots in Judaism. He founded the congregation Adat Beyt Moshe (ABM) in Philadelphia in 1951, attracting members through a weekly radio show. Having amassed eight families (fifty people), the congregation relocated in 1962 to New Jersey where they had bought a plot of land. Here, inspired by Israeli kibbutzes, they built homes and a synagogue. At some point, Respes, whose name may be of Spanish origin, claimed to be descended from Spanish Marranos. Respes began his religious path as an Israelite – perhaps associating with Prophet Cherry's congregation before forming his own – but opted to pursue Rabbinic Judaism, studying Talmud and eventually leading his congregation into Orthodox conversion in 1972. In a 1971 letter, he wrote,

> I believe that some of the black people in America are descendants of the first Jews, and because we did not retain or perpetuate Jewish traditions and teachings, we lost our identity. The whole question of black Jews today, therefore, is theoretical since no American black Jew possesses any documentary evidence of his Jewishness. Consequently, I am a proponent of Orthodox conversion as the only means by which blacks claiming to be Jews may establish the authenticity of their Jewishness. (Respes 1971)

This led to a short debate between him and Steven Jacobs (see below), who noted that Respes had taught precisely the opposite to his congregation for many

---

[22] This congregation attracted several of Ford's previous followers, although it did not comprise more than sixty members in the entirety of its existence. The congregation's Torah scroll was that brought back from Ethiopia by Eudora Paris.

[23] This Mount Horeb congregation was formed in 1964 as the merger of three different CK groups: Mount Horeb, Kohol Beth B'nai Yisrael, and Beth Emet. The Senior Rabbi was Albert Moses, assisted by Paris and Elder Matthias. It met at an Ashkenazi-owned building in the Bronx, the Young Israel Building.

years and that ABM's conversion was mandatory for their *aliyah* (immigration to Israel). Respes responded that this was true but did not change his belief in conversion. His family has remained Jews, and several of his children and grandchildren have lived in Israel (Gelman 1965; Berry 1977; E. E. 2020).

It was through Respes's radio show that Rudolph "Yehuda" Windsor (b.1935, New Jersey) first encountered BHI. Windsor studied with Respes for two years and went on to be a spiritual leader of Philadelphia's Adath Emeth Israel (AEI).[24] He visited Israel in 1970, but decided that the time was not right for any more Black *aliyah*. A self-taught historian and student of controversial Afrocentric scholar and self-proclaimed Black Jew Yosef A. A. ben Jochannan,[25] Windsor has authored several books on Hebrew Israelism/Black Jews, including the important and influential *From Babylon to Timbuktu*.[26] This text is read by Black Israelites of many different varieties and is notable for contending that Sephardic Jews, including Maimonides, are Black. He studied Hebrew Literature at Gratz College, an institution specializing in Jewish Studies located in Melrose Park, Pennsylvania. Demonstrating his interest in Judaism of all forms, he worshipped for some time with Prophet Cherry's congregation in Philadelphia as well as a Sephardic congregation. At AEI he worked closely with Rabbi Dahton Nasi (b. Dayton L. Prince, 1924–2014). Dahton was another of Respes's pupils, and later of the post-COGASOC Congregation Temple Beth El, and finally, the very similarly named Congregation Temple Bethel (Ben Levy n.d.e.; Weaver 2014).

This particular Congregation Temple Bethel (CTB) was founded in Philadelphia by Louise Elizabeth "Mother" Dailey (1918–2001) in 1956, as part of the House of God Holiness Church. Dailey was born in Annapolis, Maryland to a Baptist family, but while housekeeping for a Jewish family she recognized many of their customs as similar to those of her family. In 1976, she began a process of learning and study which slowly led Bethel away from the House of God – their cooperation ended with her ultimatum that they choose between her and Jesus; a number of members chose her. CTB is now led by her daughter, Rabbi Debra Bowen, who has significantly progressed the congregation in the direction of Rabbinic Jewish norms and traditions in practice. She

---

[24] Founded in 1968, AEI comprised 25 families, but was defunct by 1974. In a statement of goodwill, Adath Emeth Israel received a Torah scroll from a white Jewish congregation, Har Zion Temple, in 1970.

[25] Ben-Jochannan claimed Ethiopian and Puerto Rican Jewish descent, although he never participated in any congregation or practiced any form of Judaism. This assertion – as well as his purported advanced qualifications – have been judged spurious by others (Kestenbaum 2015; *Africology: Journal of Pan-African Studies* 8.10 (2016)).

[26] *From Babylon to Timbuktu* was the inspiration for Brooklyn rapper Timbo King's 2011 album *From Babylon to Timbuk2*.

identifies them as "Conservadox," between Conservative and Orthodox, although the absence of Talmudic study makes the usual definitions moot.[27] CTB does not share any roots with other BHI groups and has succeeded in integrating its beliefs and practices with those of the larger Jewish world. It is accepted as Jewish by several local congregations despite its members never having converted, and Mother Dailey is buried in a Jewish cemetery. Members prefer to be called simply Jews than any other term and reject the Black nationalist associations of BHI. In what may be the only quantitative theological survey of Hebrew Israelites, it was found that 52.8 percent of the congregation believed in a God who was "active and angry [regarding humanity's sinfulness]," an issue to which we will return in the conclusion (Gillick 2009; Ross 2009).[28]

A final figure worthy of note in this regard is Rabbi Robert Devine (1926–2019). Born in Port Gibson, Mississippi, and raised in Memphis until the age of six when his family moved to Chicago, Devine claimed his parents were BHIs, with a putative Ethiopian source. His son Azriel has refuted this, however, describing his father's roots in the Church of God in Christ before the gradual realization of his Israelite faith in his twenties. Having been expelled from the COGIC for incorporating BHI claims into his ministry, he attended Reuben's CEH, and in 1956 founded his own storefront congregation, the House of Israel Hebrew Culture Center (HOIHCC). Befriended by a curious Holocaust survivor, he learned many of the traditional Jewish practices and decided to send his children to a Conservative congregation's school. He claimed to have subsequently been converted to all three major forms of American Judaism in order to avoid doubt about his identity, although this seems to be referring to his acceptance as Jewish by the board of Conservative rabbis who interviewed him.[29] Certainly, throughout his life he considered the New Testament to be an integral part of scripture. After speaking at several Chicago synagogues through the early 1970s he was welcomed – with a little bemusement – at Milwaukee, Wisconsin's Congregation Shalom in 1973. Rabbi Bruce Diamond invited him, intending to remind his members that "our ancestors were a conglomeration of peoples, linked together by a central covenant with God." However, Devine's

---

[27] Ross (2009) argues that, with their highly spiritual and joyous approach, they are most similar to Hasidic Judaism.

[28] COGIC is a large Holiness-Pentecostal Church, from which emerged several other BHI leaders: Rabbis James Hodges (b. Mississippi 1927–2021) and Richard Nolan (later known as El Sheaknaw Levy Yisrael) – who formed a congregation with Devine. Yahweh Ben Yahweh also hailed therefrom (see below).

[29] According to the Chicago Board of Rabbis in 1973, no Hebrew Israelite had ever converted to rabbinic Judaism there. According to Azriel he passed the interview because of his training by Avihu and the advice of the Holocaust survivor.

assertions that his congregation were better Jews than their hosts, and his distribution of literature claiming that white Jews were Roman converts attracted some annoyance (*Wisconsin Jewish Herald* 1973; Chester 1974; Lewi 2009).

During the early 1960s, Devine was involved in the A-Beta Hebrew Culture Center (see Section 3), as were many of Chicago's BHIs, but he left due to disagreement with their policy of emigration. Following the example of several others before him, Devine bought 80 acres of land in Mississippi on which he established a kibbutz in 1980, partly in anticipation of the coming apocalypse. Devine was an important figure in Chicago and around the Midwest, where he helped establish many congregations in Indiana, Wisconsin, Illinois, and Michigan, as well as the first BHI organization to be recognized by the Chicago Board of Rabbis, the United Leadership Council of Hebrew Israelites (1967). He taught many future leaders and was a founding member of the Board of Black and White Rabbis along with Hodges, Nolan, Reuben, and the Chicago Conservative Beth Din. The HOIHCC still exists and is now managed by Devine's student, Rabbi Ahmetahee Malachi Yeroozedek (b. Ricky Jackson, 1962, in Canton, Mississippi).[30]

Possibly the most well-known living BHI leader was once a student of Devine: Rabbi Capers C. Funnye Jr. (b. 1952). Born in Georgetown, South Carolina, Funnye's family moved to Chicago while he was young, and although he was raised in the African Methodist Episcopal Church, he became dissatisfied with Christianity for both theological and political reasons. He did not accept the trinity and rejected especially the idea of praying to a white Jesus. His first contact with BHI was when he met Devine and began attending his HOIHCC in 1972 – which solved Funnye's theological problem not by removing Jesus but by making Jesus Black. Sometime later, however, he discovered the Israelite Rabbinic Academy in New York and, inspired by their more strictly Judaic practice, he began studying with R. Levi Ben Levy in 1980, completing his training in 1985. Remarkably, he underwent a Conservative conversion the same year, encouraged by his belief that Black and white Jews needed to come together. He earned a BA in Jewish Studies at Chicago's Spertus Institute for Jewish Learning and Leadership and would become the first African American member of the Chicago Board of Rabbis, as well as participating in other Jewish establishments. In 1995, he founded the Alliance of Black Jews, and in 2015 the Israelite Board of Rabbis made him the third Black Chief Rabbi. Although Funnye did not assert any Israelite ancestry prior to his adoption of Judaism, he recently discovered that his great-great-grandmother was named Tamara

---

[30] www.hoihcc.org.

Cohen, an unmistakably Jewish name (Kaye/Kantrowitz 2007; Kestenbaum 2015).

Funnye is the leader of Beth Shalom B'Nai Zaken EHC (BSBZEHC) of Chicago, a mixed congregation made up of BHIs, African American, Latin American, and African Jews, as well as biracial couples and Ashkenazi Jews, including some with adopted African American children. The congregation is Conservadox, with separate male–female seating but all-gender Torah readings. Upon taking leadership of Beth Shalom, Funnye recognized all existing members of the various merging congregations as Jews, but since then has insisted that all new members must either be established members of a congregation with a record of a Torah-observant lifestyle or must undergo halakhic conversion (including assessment by Chicago's Conservative Beth Din) – thereby becoming part of the Jewish community (Gillick 2009). The congregation has its own fascinating history covering more than a century, including a number of mergers with other congregations.

Official sources assert that BSBZEHC was founded in 1915, initially as the Ethiopian Hebrew Association, by an Indian Jew named Rabbi Horace Hasan, who joined forces first with Rabbis David Lazarus and Caino Stirson in 1918, then with Avihu Reuben in 1923. In 1984, it was merged with Reuben's CEH, to become Beth Shalom EHC, and then in 1993 with Congregation B'nai Zaken.[31] Since Reuben's death in 1991, it has been run solely by Funnye, with the assistance of a hierarchy that represents the different groups that joined: a Cohane (Priest), from the Righteous Branch of African Hebrews (RBAH),[32] and Nasikim/Nasikot (Princes and Princesses), from B'nai Zaken. In 1994, BSBZEHC purchased the synagogue building of a white congregation, Agudas Achim Bikur Cholim, and incorporated their remaining members. Funnye has faced some criticism from other BHIs for his willingness to blur the boundaries with white "Edomite" Judaism (see below), but this is only one aspect of the broad project which Funnye heads. His congregation is intentionally diverse, incorporating all strands of BHI and Jewish traditions; new members joining the congregation come from all kinds of backgrounds, both Hebrew Israelite and not. Funnye himself has claimed that each community of Jews must live and practice according to their own culture and history, thus his is not an attempt to abnegate all boundaries (Key 2011).

---

[31] B'nai Zaken, founded in 1952 by Prince Yaakov and Navi William Tate, was originally based in Brooklyn, and for some years had a reputation of involvement with local gangs. They changed their priorities long before the Chicago branch joined Beth Shalom, however (*New York Times* 1974).

[32] RBAH was formed by members of the AHIJ who returned from Liberia and Israel (see Section 3).

No external records support the existence of Horace Hasan, and it seems unlikely that an Indian Jew would call his congregation "Ethiopian." There was, however, a Rabbi Horace in Chicago at the time who was Black and claimed to be from Ethiopia, Somalia, or the American South, and whose surname sounded similar to "Hussein." According to Landing, this Horace led the Congregation of Israel (2002). Landing also notes that Reuben believed Rabbi Horace's full name was Horace Crowder, a suggestion he believes to be the result of confusing W. S. Crowdy and Rabbi Horace. There was in fact a Saint Horace Crowdy mentioned as part of COGASOC, who was most likely Crowdy's second cousin and brother of Joseph W. Crowdy (*Washington Post* 1906; Church of God n.d.). It is therefore not impossible that all of these Horaces were the same individual, making Rabbi Horace a relative of Crowdy and a member of COGASOC before establishing his own congregation, the Ethiopian Hebrew Association, in Chicago.

Ironically, Funnye's well-accepted congregation may have some roots in one of the most notorious BHI organizations of 1920s Harlem – Warien Roberson's Ever Live Never Die Society (ELNDS), also known as the Temple of the Gospel of the Kingdom (TGK): Lazarus and Stirson (also spelled Stifom and Stifson) were members of ELNDS who relocated to Chicago. Roberson (or Robinson, 1880–1931) remains one of the most disreputable characters in BHI. He began as a Holiness preacher, but was dogged by run-ins with the law; he was wanted in several states and served two prison sentences in New Jersey in the early decades of the twentieth century. During this time the interim leader, Doc Murphy, died in a shootout with police. Roberson's followers collected large amounts of money, including from Jews, whom they convinced through the Yiddish language and customs they hired local Jews to teach them. Roberson and his associates were sought and arrested several times in several states for a variety of crimes, most commonly fraudulent collection of money, and theft, but finally for transporting young women across state lines for (his exclusive) sexual use. In the words of Dorman, "The fiasco confirmed the poor opinion of Black sects among many African Americans as well as Jews" (Dorman 2013: 117; see also New York Age 1921; Landing 2002). Lazarus and Stirson were similarly disreputable (Broad Ax 1926; Atlanta Constitution 1926; Hernandez 1932; Koppel 2008).

Issues of Identity and Conversion

Many Rabbinic Hebrew Israelites during the twentieth century have falsely claimed Ethiopian descent. On the one hand, we can relate these attempts to "Soul Citizenship" (Markowitz et al. 2003): the creation of a historical bond that matches the spiritual one. The claim of long genetic descent is only the same authentication mechanism as many religious reformers have used, claiming that they have an unquestionably authentic source, such that their innovations appear as ancient traditions. On the other hand, we should recognize that in 1920s Harlem, many were inventing new identities and histories, passing themselves off as travelers from the Orient, India, Mecca, or Africa, or as professors, Shriners, or other respected figures, either to acquire a higher level of credibility or respect than simply being an American Black. Dorman writes,

> [T]he black Orientalist's self-presentations were earnest attempts to create new, exotic, biographies that not only would grant them the mystique to peddle religious goods in the context of African American religious and healing traditions, but also to escape Jim Crow racism and criticize the Western civilization that had brought it about. (Dorman 2004: 192)

For example, in the 1920s the Black cantor Thomas LaRue adopted the Hebraic stage name Towje Hakohen, but it was his European promoters who invented an Ethiopian backstory as a means of exoticizing him as a Black African Jew (Sapoznik 2020). Unfortunately, the patent falseness of BHIs' claims has worked against their acceptance, creating an appearance of manipulation and unreliability.

The significance of the fact that many of the leaders and members of the second wave were recent immigrants from the Caribbean should not be underestimated. Caribbean culture was considerably different from the American, and many new arrivals were shocked both by the undesirable lifestyles and deferential outlooks of poor Blacks in the cities and by the racism that was dominant in white society. Having grown up in locations lacking a white majority, and where the social position of Blacks was not that of an underclass, they were more conservative and more dignified in their bearings. Wentworth Matthew disparaged typical "Negro" behavior. Moreover, much of the Caribbean had had a relatively large Sephardic Jewish population during previous centuries, as well as a significant (even if small) mixed-race Black Jewish heritage. Even if many of those arriving in areas such as Harlem were not practicing anything recognizable as Judaism, the long cultural influence of Jewish practice – as well as the Christian Revivalism that helped produce Rastafarianism – upon the Black Christianity of those regions should not be discounted. Experiencing a distaste for the Christianity they discovered in their new locations, Caribbean immigrants undoubtedly felt the urge to differentiate themselves, and it may have led them to focus on what was more Jewish in both doctrine and practice.

In addition, here and in the third wave we see a number of adherents assert that, although they discovered Hebrew Israelism as an adult, they remembered being told by relatives that they were Hebrews or Jews. Often this came from a grandparent who was born into slavery. It is difficult to know how to interpret these statements. On the one hand, some of those claiming such ancestry have at other times denied it. Were they not so common, these declarations could easily be discounted as wishful thinking. Even accepting the veracity of these assertions, it remains unclear what they mean. Were BHIs claiming to have received oral tradition of a Hebrew lineage from Africa, which hailed from an African tribe with existing ties to Israelite heritage? The general absence of other information passed along dozens of generations makes this possibility seem unlikely. Were they referring to the connection that enslaved people felt with the Israelite experience of bondage in Egypt and Babylon? Certainly, this common trope has been picked up and taken literally by many; perhaps a literal identification was passed down prior to Crowdy and Christian. Or, were BHIs passing down stories that originated from an ancestor's enslavement in a Jewish home, and their resulting indoctrination by, identification as, and intermarriage with Jews rather than Christians?

It is largely impossible for us now to know, but in one case, a Chicago Hebrew Israelite named Yaakov Lee, in 1963, told a reporter that his great-grandmother, born enslaved in Virginia, told him that they were Hebrews but that no white person must ever know. She would refer often to *shechitah* (Jewish ritual slaughter) laws, and burnt offerings, and tried to convince the children to observe Saturday as the sabbath. His great-grandmother had further informed him that the real New Year came not in January, but in September–October (Rosenzweig 1963). This last fact indicates the highest likelihood that the last option listed above was the case, at least for Lee. His description of his great-grandmother using the Rabbinic Hebrew terms *Hashem* and *Elokeinu* also indicates a Rabbinic Jewish background.

On the other hand, Josef Ben Levi, Professor of Philosophy at Northeastern Illinois University and associate of several groups mentioned already including Brooklyn's Hashabah Yisrael, has recounted a family tradition that his grandmother's grandfather Govan was a practicing Hebrew, captured in the 1830s from Benin (private communication 10 August 2023).

One attempt to help build a relationship between Rabbinic BHI and the normative Jewish world took the form of Hatzaad Harishon (The First Step). Founded by Irving Block and Yaakov Gladstone (1923–2019), who also taught Hebrew at Mount Horeb Congregation, with Hailu Paris as a founding member, HH existed from 1964 until 1972, organizing events and meetings which were geared toward fostering communication, unity, and understanding between the two communities. Block believed that it was BHI that offered the key to defusing Black antisemitism as well as transmitting Jewish values into Black America and aiding the fight against anti-Black racism more generally.

HH's president, and another founding member, was Esther Bibbins (1932–1976), whose father-in-law Edward Meredith David Bibbins, aka Abba Bivens, would become an important figure in New York's radical BHI scene (see Section 4). Esther and her husband William Henry Chaim were members of Mount Horeb; they would later convert to Orthodox Judaism (Fernheimer 2012).[33]

A combination of factors led to the group's demise – a lack of funds, a lack of unity, and the resignation of Gladstone as Director in the summer of 1970 effectively doomed the organization. Gladstone explicitly cited the issue of conversion – the rabbinic demand and the Black refusal – as the key issue in his regretful withdrawal. His replacement, James Benjamin, was able to hold the fort for only two years as the arrival and confrontational attitude of the African Hebrew Israelites in Israel conflicted with the Israeli demand to convert or leave (see Section 3), along with the expulsion of several Black students from a yeshiva in New York due to doubts about their halakhic status, overwhelmed what good will was left (Fernheimer 2014).

Contemporaneous with HH were other organizations with the same objectives: Philadelphia's Association of Black and White Jews, organized by Steven Jacobs – a white member of AEI – and Rudolph Windsor, in 1969; and Chicago's Fellowship of Multi-Racial Jews. Neither of these appears to have lasted even as long as HH.

The issue of conversion has remained one of the most controversial and unbreachable. Rabbi Sholomo Ben Levy wrote:

> Since the particular Halakhic conversion ceremony in use today is not found in the Torah, nor is it referred to in any of the biblical instances where people joined the Hebrew faith, (Ruth for example), we do not believe that it has the same legal weight as Torah law. Also, we feel that it denies the concept of divine intervention and selection referred to in Isaiah 11:11–12 and Jeremiah 3:14. In these passages the Hebrew prophets state that God will be responsible for the gathering of His people [. . .] The fact that Orthodox rabbis hold that they are the sole arbiters of deciding who is a Jew negates the existence or exercise of a divine will that is not channelled through them first. (ben Levy n.d.h.)[34]

---

[33] Although she was born in New York, Esther's parents appear to be of Caribbean background: her mother Ruth Elizabeth Joseph from St. Kitts and her father Clisnes Joseph from Haiti.

[34] This prioritizing of Divine Will over human authority represents a significant break with rabbinic tradition, wherein humans are the sole interpreters and arbiters of the Law – a conclusion reached during the formative period of Rabbinic Judaism, most likely in order to safeguard the traditions from the danger of any "divinely inspired" radical reformers.

This theological justification elides what is likely the most pertinent issue for many Hebrew Israelites: accepting conversion by the white rabbinic establishment automatically places them in a subordinate position, not to mention one which denigrates their claim to be authentic Israelites by blood. Such a practice appears to inherently delegitimize BHI.

In addition to these issues, BHIs commonly raise the matter of observance. Put simply, if one lives a Torah-observant life, then one should not need to undergo any formal process to become part of the community and to be an Israelite. It is often noted by BHIs that, while they strictly uphold the Mosaic Law and are not considered Jews, white Jews are regarded as Jews even while the majority of them do not keep the Law, or pick and choose which parts they believe are important. If these lax, and even atheist, white Jews are still accepted as Jews then surely their highly observant and committed Black brethren should be? For the rabbinate, however, *halakhah* decrees that performance is a religious requirement of the people of Israel, but the two are not equivalent; this is to say, even a lax Jew is still a Jew, and a non-Jew who performs the same rituals is still a non-Jew until they undergo formal conversion. There are certainly cases where allowances have been made, and the fact that such allowances had sometimes been made for small European communities in the past gave the appearance of racism. (Communities such as the Subbotnik, for example, were accepted on the basis of their centuries-long commitment to Judaism and their shared persecution by the Nazis). Indeed, Andre Key has cited several aspects of *halakhah* recently repealed by even the Masorti (Modern Orthodox) rabbinate, claiming that this demonstrates the racism behind maintaining a strict approach to Jewish boundaries (Key 2023a).

However, from the other side, we might also recognize an irony in Rabbinic Hebrew Israelites' resentment regarding nonacceptance by an establishment which they believe is essentially lacking in ultimate authority and in their indignation at nonacceptance – yet refusal to engage in the required process. For BHIs, this is a point of principle, whereas for the rabbinate it is a concern about absorbing elements that are intentionally contrary to Jewish tradition. It cannot be ignored that, while Rabbinic BHIs perceive their rejection by Jews as racism, many still hold that white Jews are descended from Esau, the biblical brother of Jacob who was "hated" by God and whose descendants formed the biblical paradigm of human evil. This motif is deep in the tradition–history, being advocated by Wentworth Matthew. While Rabbinic BHIs do not ascribe an evil nature to modern Jews, other BHI groups do, and the Rabbinic BHIs do not provide any clear boundary between themselves and the more radical elements of their broader community. This clearly presents a great difficulty to the Jewish establishment.

While Matthew gave up on seeking the white Jewish world's acceptance in the mid-1960s, one of his students attempted – and to some degree succeeded – in finding it. Rabbi Dr. Chakwal Morton Cragg (b. Christopher M. Cragg, 1924) claimed that his father was Ethiopian and his paternal grandfather was of Ethiopian Jewish descent. He says that he decided to pursue his Jewish roots after experiencing a lack of prejudice from Jewish soldiers he fought with in the Second World War. The latter is more likely than the former, given that his grandfather's birth is recorded as Virginia, 1850, and the family were practicing Baptists. Although Matthew trained him, Cragg came to reject what he considered Matthew's "racial chauvinism," and founded the Union of EHCs and Rabbis (UEHCR) – the first Black body to be accepted into the Union of American Hebrew Congregations. Consisting of Cragg, the white Jewish Martin J Warmbrand (1926–2019, who would later become President of the Pro-Falasha Committee), and some others, the UEHCR elected Taamrat Emmanuel as Honorary President – much to his surprise, although he graciously accepted the position offered by people he had "unfortunately never known." (Emmanuel 1955) Cragg's own interracial Temple Society of Ethiopian Hebrews, which he designated "Falasha Jewry's first liberal congregation," was accepted in the Reconstructionist movement, and later renamed the Harlem Reconstructionist Synagogue. Cragg also edited *The African Israelite*, seemingly the first publication for "colored Jewry," a bimonthly paper produced for roughly ten years from 1955 which was "devoted to Klal Yisroel, the abolition of antisemitism among persons of color, Eretz Yisroel, the Falashas and other Jews of color the world over." Despite developing an impressive profile during the late 1950s, Cragg disappeared after this.[35] Although Cragg apparently did not convert, he was nevertheless accepted by the establishment. Like Dailey and Devine, he was accepted as a Jew simply based on his knowledge and commitment to rabbinic traditions. It is perhaps important to remember that Matthew himself was not rejected as a Jew, but simply as one whose knowledge and training did not meet the criteria for a rabbi.

Martin Warmbrand, noted above, authored an early article on Black Jews (Warmbrand 1969), and in 1965 told a reporter,

> I am incensed by those headline-seeking reporters who seem to be exclusively interested in unearthing off-beat sects of individual charlatans masquerading as Jews. Some of the black Jews [...] have never known another

---

[35] The only real record of Cragg's achievements is the Chakwal Morton Cragg papers, SC-8792. American Jewish Archives, Cincinnati, Ohio. https://7079.sydneyplus.com/archive/final/Portal/AmericanJewishArchives.aspx?component=AABC&record=50738b42-1e5b-46c9-9db3-9ae4668aa0df. Several specifically BHI publications have since been started, including the *Jerusalem Chronicle* (founded by Yehoshaphat Israel in 1989), and the Torah-only focused *Hebrew Israelite Nation Times*, http://hint-magazine.com/ (founded by Tyrone Webb in 2014).

religion. They practice the Jewish faith as they were taught at home by their parents [. . .] For them there is no religion but Judaism. (Cohen 1965: 14)

Indeed, the same article describes significant interest and sympathy from all sectors of the Jewish community. Israel Klavan, Executive Vice President of the Orthodox Rabbinical Council of America, stated that they are "particularly" interested "in the effort to assist Jews who also happen to be Negroes, in every possible way" (Cohen 1965: 3).

The difficulties, then, were clearly not to do with race in the simple sense, although the issue does demonstrate the insidiousness of structural racism. As Fernheimer (2014) described, the problem during the period of attempted reconciliation of the late 1960s and early 1970s, was one of framing and communication. Hebrew Israelites were thinking in terms of race, while the Jewish establishment was thinking in terms of religious tradition. The establishment stuck fast to its principle that no one was Jewish unless they had been converted or were born to a recognized Jewish mother. The Israelites were adamant that they were of the latter category and were only being questioned because of their Blackness. Effectively, the Jewish establishment said, "We are happy to accept you as Jews as long as you fit our criteria for Jewishness." While this criteria had no explicit racial barrier, it still was embedded in the white Jewish establishment which saw its own narrative, history, and structure as the only valid Judaism. Therefore, there was arguably a structural racism built into it. The Israelites believed firmly that their own claims were of at least equal legitimacy as those of the white establishment, and they would not agree to subsume themselves under another structure which claimed to be the only true path. Clearly, these two conflicting narratives could not be resolved, and so the attempts at reconciliation, on the macro-scale, failed.

The final words of this section go to Rabbi Sholomo Ben Levy:

Like our great founder, we have a deep respect and admiration for every other Jewish community. We continue to learn and benefit from the treasures of knowledge that are available to us. However, Rabbi Matthew also understood that those who Hashem are bringing back as He promised to do through the words of the prophets, have a special role to play in the ultimate restoration of Israel. As such, we are not empty vessels before a full fountain; i.e., a people who enters Judaism with nothing to contribute. On the contrary, we have the spirit that will breath new life into the dry bones. We bring an innate intelligence that allows us to understand and apply Torah to the world in which we live. We occupy a special place in the heart of the Creator, the lost child who has been found and returned. And, we bring a creativity and an independence that allows us to shape and mold our own culture, songs, dress, and traditions from all the sources that make up our identity. (Ben Levy n.d.g.)

3 Third Wave: 1960s Midwest

The leaders and congregations that came of age during the Second World War and the massive ruptures that emerged in American society thereafter make up the third wave. They were the contemporaries of Emmett Till, saw the end of Jim Crow legislation and the achievements – and failings – of the civil rights movement led by Martin Luther King Jr. They had seen Elijah Muhammad turn the NOI into a potent force in America's cities, with a new vision of Black pride and autonomy. They were witnessing the independence of many African and Asian states, revolutions which suggested that a new era was dawning. They were motivated to achieve, yet painfully aware of their status in American society and of the threats that surrounded them.

It is here that we see the clear divorce between the BHI and Rabbinic Judaism. A number of factors combined to produce this result. Black Power's assertiveness and a new Afrocentrism led to the creation of Israelite identities which were intentionally distinct from that of the so-called white Jewish establishment. This included the clothing which shifted from the conservative and Masonic-influenced dress of the first two waves to African styles, with a revised perspective on Jewish ritual adornment, such as head coverings and fringes (Key 2023b). We also cannot separate this schism from the swiftly growing gulf between Blacks and Jews who had previously been largely allied. At this point, Jews were becoming fully accepted into the white strata of American society by both whites and Blacks. The Israeli occupation of the West Bank and Gaza after the 1967 war, which sealed Israel's status as a regional power with colonial overtones and American support, did little to alter the perception of Jewish whiteness and participation in the oppression of darker peoples. At the same time, the white Jewish leadership of organizations like the National Association for the Advancement of Colored People (NAACP), the Urban League, and other organizations, was popularly rejected. Meanwhile, the New York teachers' strike of 1968 saw white teachers and principals who were often Jewish dismissed from largely Black schools.[36]

Despite the undeniable influence of Black Power and Afrocentrism upon the developments in BHI's third wave, the primacy of Blackness was always a part of the movement. We also cannot ignore the influence of early pro-Black, proto-Afrocentric writers such as Jamaican journalist and popular historian J. A. Rogers, who in the early decades of the twentieth century argued for the originality of Black humans and the influence of early African civilizations upon the West. These thinkers were self-taught but wrote with a learned and

---

[36] Although see Kaye/Kantrowitz's discussion of the problematic tendency to reduce Black-Jewish relations to an antagonistic binary (2007: 51–7).

professional style which garnered readers among the growing Black intelligent-sia. That Hebrew Israelites and their leaders were consuming such material is beyond doubt.

Our first leader of this more separatist brand of Hebrew Israelism is Lucius Casey Sr. (1903–1978). Born in Mississippi, Casey was illiterate, largely uneducated, and suffered a serious speech impediment. He moved to Chicago in the 1940s with his wife and son, to escape both unemployment and violent southern racism. Initially, he had to support his family by selling rags but later found work as a janitor. He taught himself to read at age thirty-eight, in order to read the Bible and find the reasons why God had let Blacks be so badly treated. From this study, he realized his spiritual calling. He started preaching on the streets of Chicago and formed the Israelite Bible Study Group.[37] He opposed integration and rejected the New Testament except for Revelation. In 1953, the Bible Study group purchased 944 acres of farmland near Ullin, southern Illinois, where Casey and his 400 followers would wait for Armageddon, which they expected to arrive within the decade (Stewart 1966). Casey taught that as the nations went to war in the Middle East, all would be destroyed, leaving only the righteous Israelites, along with some whites who might survive as servants. As a result, the Israelite Farm had to become self-sufficient, so as to provide for themselves after the tribulation, and their rapturous transportation to the Promised Land. As members arrived with their mobile homes, they gradually built up the land, constructing dwellings, roads, and a playground. They even constructed their own sewage system. The group filed for tax-exempt status in 1973 under the name First Church of Israel, but due to the failure to file annual reports, it did not obtain it. The name change caused internal disputes and the organization split into Bible Class and First Church communities, although it is unclear what differences they held apart from their preferred name. After Casey's death, the community could not agree on who would be his successor. Problems only worsened, leading to the eviction of six members of the First Church faction, who subsequently filed a $4 million lawsuit to regain their homes. The lawsuit failed. By 2008, there were only a dozen people left on the Israelite Farm, although thirty members lived nearby and visited for weekly services – which the two camps held separately.

Casey's community still exists on the Israelite Farm near Ullin, where they live quiet lives and maintain their beliefs; they seem to have dropped their opposition to integration since their children attend a local school. According to Alonzia Harris, who joined the group in 1964, and has lived on the farm since

---

[37] There is also a report from the 1960s of a group called the Children of Israel, founded by Casey, with branches in several states.

1979, "The New Testament was written by the white man to brainwash us. We got his education, his philosophy, and his way of life, as well. We have been living in darkness because of the New Testament." Illustrating the nationalist impulse that attracted many in the 1960s, he continued: "We are the only race of people without a homeland. We don't have a flag, do we? If you ask a Chinese where he's from, he'll say China. Ask a Japanese, he'll say Japan. Ask a German, he'll say Germany. Ask a black person, what can he say? [...] We are from the land of Israel. That's our home" (Murphy 1980; Perkins 1983; Southern Illinoisan 1983: 6; Blythe 1989; George 2008).

From Casey's Israelite Bible Class came another generation of Hebrew Israelites in Chicago, who would push his teachings into new territory.

One of those who attended Casey's Bible Study meetings was Ben Ammi (b. Ben Carter, 1939–2014). Born in Chicago, Ammi began accompanying his workmate Eliyahu (Leonard) Buie to meetings in the early 1960s. There were many Israelite groups in Chicago at the time, and Ammi helped to found a new, putatively umbrella, organization: the A-Beta Hebrew Culture Center. The venture attracted many leading figures in Chicago's Israelite scene, including the elders Avihu Reuben and Robert Devine, and Naphtali Israel (who taught Hebrew). They actively proselytized and became well known in Black Chicago. A-Beta's first publication was the pamphlet "The American Negro in Bible Prophecy" (1966), featured in the photograph *Culture* by Chicago Black Arts Movement photographer Robert Crawford, where it is held proudly by a woman along with "Return to Africa her Stolen Children" (Pittsburgh Courier 1967; Crawford 2006).

Emigration quickly became a core point of A-Beta's platform, leading older and more conservative members such as Reuben and Divine to leave the group. In 1967, more than 150 members made their way to Liberia, where they purchased land and began farming. This venture was beset by difficulties: the hard life, many miles from the nearest city, the lack of funds for essentials, and the combative flora and fauna of the Liberian jungle convinced many to return to America (some would end up in Funnye's Beth Shalom), although almost as many new recruits replaced them. Taking Martin Luther King's last speech – where he claimed to have seen the Promised Land that Black Americans as a people would reach – as a prophetic sign, in late 1969 small groups began to fly to Israel. Thereafter, they became known as the Original Black Hebrew Israelite Nation (colloquially Black Hebrews).

The 1970s and 1980s in Israel were difficult for the group. They maintained a war of attrition with the state, which did not accept them as Jews and, after the group's rejection of the conversions offered to them, attempted to deport them. Members likewise rejected Israeli authority and Jewish legitimacy, and their numbers grew from hundreds to thousands as new members arrived, disguised as Christian pilgrims. But in the late 1980s, a thaw began which led to negotiations between Israel, the Black Hebrews, and the United States, resulting in the community being granted temporary resident status in return for a commitment to bring no further members into Israel. Normalization gradually followed, with permanent resident status granted in 2003 and the option of citizenship becoming available in 2009. Members serve in the Israel Defense Forces and have become a celebrated national community, numbering about 2,500 in Israel with a similar membership abroad (Esensten 2019). They now generally prefer to be known as AHIJ or, indicating their belief that the Messianic Age has begun, the Kingdom of Yah. Africa – and the identification of Israel as part of Africa – is fundamental to their global outlook (Markowitz 1996).

The group's prior charges of Jewish inauthenticity were rescinded in 1987. However, members see their own community as at the forefront of the present era, and as those ordained to lead humanity out of the chaotic end of the Gentile Age into the Messianic Age. They consider themselves the spiritual leaders of humanity who are building the Kingdom of God in the Holy Land, which will produce the wisdom from which all of humanity will enter a new way of life (Michaeli 2000; Singer 2000; Jackson 2013).

The AHIJ tries to provide for its members' needs internally. A portion of the community's food is self-farmed, and many food products are available for sale around Israel, in addition to being consumed by the community. Clothing is produced, according to their interpretation of the biblical guidelines. Members run many other businesses, intended partly to keep the community's finances circulating internally. Income is pooled and all members' basic living expenses are paid centrally.

Ben Ammi was the community's principal theologian, his eleven books and countless lectures having set out his conception of history, truth, God, humanity, and society. All of these beliefs are sourced in the Hebrew Bible, but the influence of previous generations of BHI and African American thought is clearly discernible (Miller 2023c). Ben Ammi's status as Messiah has evolved from that of a near-identification with God to his standing as one of many anointed leaders sent to Israel throughout history.

The AHIJ's creation of governance and institutional structures goes beyond what any other groups have achieved. They have an impressive network in African states, where they contribute to community, construction, environmental, and preventive healthcare projects, through their African Hebrew Development Agency. New leaders are trained in the School of the Prophets. There still exists the tiered administrative structure Ammi created: the Holy Council of twelve Princes (*Nasik* in Hebrew) is supported by twelve Ministers

(*Sar*), each with a specific portfolio – economics, information, agriculture, education, sports, and so on. Crowned Brothers and Sisters (*atar/atarah,* the only leadership tier to include females) are the point of regular contact for members (Jackson 2013).

The AHIJ mandates conservative social roles, the eradication of feminism, homosexuality, drug use, unrighteous entertainment, and unrighteous lifestyles. The family is the basic unit of the community, which is structured patriarchally, although husbands are commanded to listen to the input of their wives when making decisions. Women are educated and often work as well as take care of the home. The community practices Divine Marriage, wherein a man may marry up to seven wives, depending on his ability to support them. This is justified by appeal to biblical figures such as David, and some African tribal traditions. However a minority of marriages are polygynous, and very few consist of more than two wives (Markowitz 2000).

Since 1973, the AHIJ has been entirely vegan. This is based on its reading of Genesis 1:29, where God gives to Adam and Eve "every seed-bearing plant on the face of the whole earth and every tree that has fruit with seed in it. They will be yours for food." Veganism and a health-centered approach to life are core principles and a central part of what the group presents to the world. Participants have opened several vegan restaurants in Israel, the United States, and Africa. Members also do not consume any intoxicants, including tobacco, alcohol (except for especially brewed wine, during festivals), and caffeine. As well as spending three days every week eating only raw food, they have progressively instituted new annual dietary restrictions based on scientific guidance. Every member is expected to exercise three times per week. This emphasis on reclaiming the "Edenic" life culminates in the overcoming of death through physical immortality (Markowitz and Avieli 2020; Miller 2023a).

Despite some predictions of apocalyptic violence, the AHIJ has always rejected violence as a means of achieving its goals, and in 2005 the Dr. Martin Luther King Jr./SCLC-Ben Ammi Institute for a New Humanity, a research center for the study of nonviolence was opened in Dimona.

Having introduced the most significant group that emerged from the turbulent 1960s to 1970s, we must consider some groups that took the same background to a different, and more violent conclusion. The following will examine several groups contemporary with the AHIJ, but which helped to create a very negative impression of Hebrew Israelites when they came to light in the 1980s.

Contemporary with A-Beta, a second group also emerged from Lucius Casey's teachings. The House of Judah was founded in 1965 in Grand Junction, Michigan by William A. Lewis (aka Prophet David Israel, b. ca. 1922). As a child in Alabama, Lewis heard the story his grandmother had recalled of her capture in Africa. In addition, Lewis himself witnessed the beatings and murders of several Blacks in the South. After serving in the US Army during World War II, Lewis moved to Chicago with his wife and worked as an appliance repairman. In Chicago, he began to reflect on the condition of his people in America and initially dabbled in the NOI, before hearing Casey preaching on the streets. He joined Casey's group, the Children of Israel, which from the 1950s had been teaching that integration was against God's law. Later studying with Avihu Reuben, he came to believe that the suffering of Blacks was their own responsibility, and whites were being used by God to punish them. Logically, the way out of oppression then was strict adherence to the Bible.

By 1980, Lewis was living on disability payments and his House of Judah counted some seventy followers. Some of these followers lived in Chicago, but many lived in the camp they had established in Allegan County, Michigan in 1971. Lewis spoke out against integration and declared that both whites and Africans would have to serve the Israelites that together they had helped enslave for 1,000 years. Lewis hated the leadership of both Martin Luther King and Malcolm X, as well as most "irresponsible" Blacks and whites, repeatedly praised the Ku Klux Klan (KKK) as a righteous organization that kept Blacks from committing more crimes, and considered white Jews to be devils who were destroying America. Like Casey, Lewis was expecting the apocalypse imminently and held a basically Christian theological framework. Always noted for their penchant for corporal punishment – members had to sign a contract agreeing to be beaten, burned, hanged, or stoned if they broke the rules – the community became famous when a twelve-year-old boy was beaten to death in July 1983. Sixty-six other children were removed from the camp as a result, eleven of them requiring medical help. The child's mother and two others were convicted of child cruelty. By 1985 most of the camp – around 100 people – had moved to Wetumpka, Alabama. Inspired by the airlift of Ethiopian Jews to Israel, Lewis began enquiring whether the same could be done for him and his followers. But in November, he and six other leaders were arrested on charges of conspiring to hold the group's children in slavery. They were found guilty in September 1986 and the following month Lewis closed the camp, before being sentenced to three years in jail (Cogswell 1981; Bowles 1983; Standish 1983; Sznajderman 1985; Landing 2002).

Another one-time follower of Casey would help to take his teaching across state lines. Hananiah Elkanah Israel (b. Stephen Holiman in Nashville, 1905–1980) had joined Reuben's CEH in 1940 and later studied with Casey before taking the message on the road. He followed Casey's anti-integration stance and taught that both civil rights leaders and the Black Church were evil. Israel left

Chicago for Cincinnati in 1958 and one of his first followers was Elesha Yisrael (b. Carl Thomas, 1943–2012). With Daniel Yisrael, they founded the House of Yisrael in 1963. Hananiah Israel left when Elesha Yisrael became convinced that Jesus was not the Messiah, and the New Testament was not scripture. Subsequently, Elesha and Daniel founded separate Bible Study classes. Elesha taught also on the radio and cable TV and established several House of Yisrael congregations in other cities and states. In 1995, Elesha and Daniel together started a new, Torah-only, House of Yisrael, which is still in operation today.[38] They have organized an annual Sacred Law Conference, at which BHIs from around the globe have converged since 1994 (Willis 2021).

The published work of Elesha YisraEL (2014) is sparse and unforgiving. Based on a strict, although selective, biblical literalism, he proposes the destruc-tion of the unrighteous, the coming of an earthly kingdom, and sees white skin as a sign of sin, while viewing several biblical patriarchs as perfect. He also presents a motif of gender equality, arguing that the Hebrew Bible, in contrast to the New Testament, endorses female religious leaders. Much of his writing is taken up with the rejection of Christ.

The militant teachings of Hananiah Yisrael would have a tragic effect. In 1974, Alberta King, mother of Martin Luther King Jr., and one other individual were murdered by Marcus Wayne Chenault (1951–1995). Chenault had studied briefly with Hananiah and the attack was intended to target Alberta's husband, King Sr. because of his Christianity. Chenault had formed a six-person study group, but the other members recalled that he had always asserted that all vengeance was in God's hands (Sapulkas 1974).

There have been several other BHI organizations named the House of Israel. One founder was responsible for at least four such groups: Rabbi Edward Emmanuel Washington (b. David Hill in Arkansas, 1928–2005). Described by Cleveland journalist Dick Peery as "the very best conman I've ever met," (Frazier n.d.) Hill was a Church of Christ pastor and civil rights activist who, while imprisoned in 1953, came to see the true identity of Blacks as Israel. He abandoned the ideology of integration as well as Christianity. He founded his first HOI in Chicago in 1956, and then another in Cleveland, Ohio (where he was in contact with Hananiah). After being found guilty of extortion and corporate blackmail related to the Operation Black Unity protests, he fled bail in 1971, arriving in Guyana in 1972, where he founded another HOI and recruited local Afro-Guyanese. This HOI, numbering 1,500 to 2,000 members – although they claimed 8,000 – taught the now expected mixture of apocalyptic,

---

[38] House of Yisrael, http://houseofyisrael.org/. Elesha's student Mowreh Ishyah Yisrael leads a branch in Philadelphia: https://houseofyisraelphilly.org/.

anti-white, Black Israel rhetoric, mixed with Marxism. It also operated a paramilitary force for the ruling Peoples' National Congress (PNC) party. The group is implicated in the murder of at least two prominent critics, including activist and academic Walter Rodney. Rabbi Washington proclaimed himself God, but as soon as the PNC was ousted, he was arrested and sentenced to fifteen years for the murder of one of his followers in 1986. Released in 1992 he returned to the United States and opened his last HOI in Newark, New Jersey (Van Bennekom 1979; Frazier 2012; Guyana Chronicle 2014).

At the same time that the House of Judah was in the public eye and the AHIJ was undergoing the worst of their persecution in Israel, matters were complicated by the unsavory activities of another Black nationalist Hebrew Israelite group: the Temple of Yahweh (also known as the Nation of Yahweh – NOY – and the Temple of Love). Headquartered in Miami and led by Yahweh Ben Yahweh (b. Hulon Mitchell Jr. in Oklahoma, 1935–2007), the "Yahwehs," as they were called, reached 12,000 members at their peak, making them one of the most visible groups of the 1980s. The group still exists, but under the rule of Mitchell, it was only ten years before multiple murders – not to mention financial irregularities, sexual abuse, and coercive control of members – were linked to its members. Due to Ben Yahweh's frequent name changes, I will refer to him by his birth name.

Mitchell had been raised in the Church of God in Christ, where his father was a deacon, and entered the US Air Force when he was nineteen. He was well-educated, with qualifications in psychology and economics, but with a religious passion which at times convinced him he was divine. In the late 1950s or early 1960s, he campaigned against segregation with the NAACP, but soon soured on the ideal of integration. He joined the NOI and rose quickly through the ranks, taking over the Atlanta temple in 1965, but left two years later, following allegations of financial and sexual improprieties. He worked for a few years as a Christian preacher, Father Michel, garnering more than 200 loyal followers before the church disbanded and the members sued Mitchell for fraud in 1978.

By this time, Mitchell was living in Miami, and beginning a new fascination with Hebrew Israelism, using a variety of names – Brother Love, then Moses Israel, followed by Yahshua (i.e., Jesus), and finally Yahweh Ben Yahweh. Mitchell taught that the ongoing tribulations of Blacks in America, which were particularly palpable in Miami as it suffered a wave of police violence, foreshadowed the imminent apocalyptic reckoning, after which the true Israel would return to the Promised Land. The Israelites were Black, as was Yahweh – the "Great, Good and Terrible Black God." Christianity was a slave religion, imposed on Blacks by the white man. Mitchell's followers lived communally, pooling their money and possessions, keeping the Mosaic Law, while also foregoing the luxuries of alcohol, tobacco, drugs, artificial additives, gambling, and even television. Gender roles were heavily prescribed, as was the expectation of high fertility, from the onset of puberty. Financial and sexual abuse of followers began again, as did beatings for any misdemeanor; troublesome members were executed. Explicit hatred of whites was taught, they were randomly targeted for murder, a sort of rite of passage for Mitchell's inner circle, who removed one ear from the victim as proof of their crime. As the NOY spread its operation to other states in the early 1980s, it began producing Yahweh brand beer, wine, and soda (the former of which members were forbidden to drink), as well as clothing, cosmetics, and haircare, literature, records/tapes, and even children's coloring books.[39] Many other associated businesses cropped up to earn funds for the Temple, including jewelry, recording studios, and cassettes and books of Mitchell's lectures. Mitchell's followers, despite their labor, lived in near poverty. By 1990, the NOY had some $9 million in assets and some 20,000 followers, although the group itself asserted far higher, at $250 million. This figure, while surely inflated, may be closer to the truth than $9 million, given the strings of apartment complexes, hotels, stores, and a fleet of Rolls Royces the group amassed.

From 1985, Mitchell seems to have wished to change the appearance of the group. He introduced more women into positions of power, bought an old church and turned it into a school, and preached a gospel of self-reliance, hard work, and law and order. Devils were now the immoral of every race, not simply all whites. His followers successfully cleared several areas of gangs and drugs, efforts which won him the respect of many in the establishment; his charisma also helped. However, behind this façade, much remained the same. The conviction of several members of the New York branch for child abuse in 1986 demonstrated this.[40]

Lauding Mitchell as an upstanding citizen, businessman, and positive role model for Black youth, Miami Mayor Xavier Suarez declared October 7, 1990, "Yahweh ben Yahweh Day," just one month before Mitchell was indicted for conspiracy to commit murder, along with several of his followers. He was convicted and sentenced to eighteen years in 1992, but was released in 2001, with parole restrictions preventing him from making any contact with his congregation. Fifteen other members were convicted with him, and dozens of ex-members testified for the prosecution. He died in 2007, of prostate cancer (Freedberg 1994; Amani 2007; Mock 2007).

---

[39] A catalogue, *The World of Yahweh,* is preserved in Tulane University's Nation of Yahweh collection.

[40] Yesher Israel and ten others were sentenced on more than 100 charges including coercion and assault.

It is with the Black nationalist form of Hebrew Israelism described in this section, that we can most clearly see the similarities with Black Islam. Indeed, the groups discussed here evince many similarities with the NOI, which had its heyday in the 1960s. We should therefore recognize that both movements emerged from the same context – of racial oppression and poverty – and provided the same reassurances – self-belief, a strong historical identity, and a sense of responsibility, including strict discipline and righteous living – to members. Shared elements include an imminent apocalyptic expectation, set either during the 1970s or in the year 2000, often involving a nuclear holocaust; a dualistic cosmology which placed them in the center of a battle between good and evil, wherein whites were ontologically evil; a firm separatism based on Black pride and economic empowerment; antisemitism; often strict dietary guidelines going above and beyond what is in scripture (commonly advocating vegetarianism for its health benefits); the perception of Christianity as a slave religion designed to subjugate Blacks; a relocation of Heaven and Hell as this-worldly realities; and a rejection of the dualist metaphysics of matter and spirit.

The third wave is the most literary; many leaders took advantage of inexpensive printing establishments. Mitchell's first book, *You Are Not a Nigger: Our True History, the World's Best Kept Secret* (Israel 1981), aptly displays his militancy and his passion, as well as his immersion in African American religious thought from across the Abrahamic spectrum. Mitchell is probably the only such religious leader to have been equally immersed in Black Christianity, Islam, and Judaism. The text displays some conceptual similarities with Ben Ammi's thought, as laid out first in *God, the Black Man and Truth* (1982), and both absorb the NOI doctrines noted above. While sharing the Black theological tradition's special place for Blacks in the future, Mitchell is most outspoken regarding Rabbinic Jews and Zionism, describing them as "False imposter Jews [who] are in our land today." Ammi, despite some heated public statements, never committed to writing any rejection of Jews, although other AHIJ members did, e.g. Ben Yehuda 1975 – a text since deleted by the community.

Indeed, Ben Ammi is notably gentler and more subtle in his public voice. While he and Mitchell, like Muhammad, posit a cosmic struggle between the forces of good and evil in which whites fulfill the latter role, in Ammi whites are not ontologically evil, but are used by God as a rod of correction; both reject Western education as a means of integrating into a world of inequality, and their dietary regulations are very similar. They maintain a similar literalism regarding FBI Director Edgar J. Hoover's prediction of "a 'Messiah' who could unify, and electrify, the militant black nationalist movement" (FBI 1968: 2), and both surely believed it prophesied themselves. While Mitchell held that the Bible contained the history of Blacks, which whites had tried to conceal from them, he also – somewhat strangely – taught that the King James Version (KJV) was the sole dependable version of that Bible. For Ammi too, the Bible is Black history, and he favored the style of the KJV while advising the use of the Hebrew to avoid the many mistranslations and Europeanisms. Like Casey, Mitchell taught that whites would ultimately serve as slaves to Black Israelites. This element is not present in Ammi, although he does offer the more subtle claim that the wicked who made this world Hell would suffer equally living in a Heavenly world of righteousness. Indeed, where Mitchell's theology is one of vengeance, Ammi's is one of leadership: the BHIs are now taking their place in the Holy Land to lead all of humanity into Heaven.

Ammi also provides a more sophisticated theology of vitalism and immanence, understanding God as a spirit that does not intervene in the world directly, instead inhabiting human beings and guiding them toward righteous thoughts and actions, thereby providing the righteousness which sustains the world. This is effected through adherence to Mosaic Law. Opposing God is satan (which Ammi never capitalizes), the negative spiritual power which influences humans toward actions which are destructive, of both humans and the created world generally (Miller 2023c).

One strange feature of Mitchell's text is that the final chapter reproduces several pages of the "King Alfred Plan," wherein it is treated as if it were factual. This fictional CIA plan for the containment and extermination of Blacks, developed for a novel by African American author John A. Williams, formed part of a viral publicity stunt for the novel when printouts of it were left on the New York subway in October 1967. Outraged panic was the result, although its true status and source were quickly revealed (Emre 2017). The Plan was reproduced even in the most recent (1994) edition of Mitchell's text, supplemented with an extract from Samuel F. Yette's *The Choice: The Issue of Black Survival in America* (1971), which argued that the American government was already implementing a planned genocide of African Americans.

Mitchell's proclivity for sex, violence, and money all point toward a somewhat cynical personality in contrast with Ben Ammi. Despite this, Mitchell's writings display a passion and an intimate knowledge of the Bible and the religious doctrines and interpretations developed within Black America which defuses suspicions that he was simply a charlatan.

Acceptance of the New Testament varies in the third-wave groups: some strictly reject it, some see it as secondary to the Hebrew Bible, and some hold it as an integral part of scripture. Mitchell argued that the story of Jesus was the prophecy of his own life. The AHIJ considers the New Testament to be inspired recordings, but not infallible; in any cases of scriptural contradictions, preference is given to the Hebrew Bible.

Some parallel organizations and texts are worth noting. Philadelphia's Beth Hephzibah (BH) was founded by George A. Chatwick (later Ahdahm Ben Yisrael, 1925–1988) and Louis Swan (1894–1943), under the tutelage of Leon Pumphrey. Pumphrey himself was likely a Crowdyite, but BH became an "extension" of the AHIJ/KOY. Chatwick published *The Lost Nation (The So Called "Negro")* in 1974, which shares all the common features of BHI literature: dependence on Deuteronomy 28 and Ezekiel 37; rejection of white religions; rejection of the term Negro; identification of Jews with Edom; and emphasis on the Mosaic Law. It is unclear what role Jesus plays in Chatwick's thought, but he briefly cites the New Testament.

At roughly the same time as A-Beta, the Camp of the Lost and Found Sheep of the House of Israel was operative in Chicago. Their publication, *Israel's Truth Crying in the Wilderness of North America and Africa* (1970), invokes many of the same concepts as Ben Ammi, Mitchell, and Casey: whites as Edomite devils, Jews as the Synagogue of Satan, rejection of Christianity as a paganized slave religion and its preachers as conmen, rejection of the civil rights movement and democracy, belief in separatism, salvation only for Israel, America as Hell, soon to be destroyed in an imminent nuclear holocaust, and the sabbath age of the 7,000th year when God will return the Israelites to their land. It also predicts several exegetical maneuvers of the fourth-wave One West camps. Moreover, it seems to share Casey's adherence to the Hebrew Bible plus the book of Revelation.

One last group can be mentioned here – The Israelite Nation Worldwide Ministries. Run by Guyana-born Shadrock Porter (aka Nicky Porter, b.1950), it is unique in being based outside the United States, in Toronto, Canada with branches in New York, Atlanta, East Saint Louis, IL, St. Louis, MO, and London (Porter 1990). Shadrock's history is unclear: he claims his grandfather impressed both his Congolese and Israelite heritage upon him. He was a popular singer in Guyana and worked for the government before moving to Toronto. It is then strange that he doesn't mention the House of Israel or Hashaba Yisrael, as he would certainly have known of these groups.

Violence and State Concern

It was with the third wave that alarm bells began ringing. In October 1999, the FBI issued a report titled *Project Megiddo*, describing potential domestic terrorist threats as the millennium approached. Among the five categories of extremists considered were "radical fringe members" of BHI groups, in which the NOY and the AHIJ were explicitly mentioned. While the latter was considered "generally peaceful, if somewhat controversial" (FBI 1999: 24), the NOY case showed that violence could be instigated from BHI circles. The analysis drew on previous reports, including by the Anti-Defamation Leage (ADL) (1987), the SPLC (1997), and the Naval Criminal Investigative Service (1999), which informed of potential BHI threats. *Project Megiddo* did not cite any specific incidents and certainly overstated the danger in comparison to far-right extremists. Even in those BHI groups that use extreme language and rhetoric, mirroring that of the Bible, the vast majority do so without any intention of engaging in such behavior themselves. The cases cited by the FBI, while tragic for those involved, had at that point very rarely affected individuals outside of the organizations in question.

The fact that the FBI had overstated its case is clear: there were no such millennial incidents.[41] In fact, only a few weeks into 2000 one NOY member threatened a class action libel lawsuit for $12 trillion against the SPLC and ADL for their contribution to the report's defamation and demonization of members. They argued that *Project Megiddo* amounted to a hate crime against them. The fact that their leader was then serving jail time did nothing to dispel their anger – this too was supposedly part of the "war" against them. They suggested that the prosecution's witnesses were government agents, responsible for all of the murders. While denying the charge of anti-whiteness, the lawsuit itself engages in explicit antisemitism, casting Jews as the Synagogue of Satan and as the controllers of "the publishing and entertainment industries, the educational and judicial systems, and all other businesses and professions of this world" (Southern Poverty Law Center n.d.a.; Nation of Yahweh n.d.).

Manipulative and violent leaders who control their followers and convince them to commit crimes are of course not unique to BHI. Such leaders and groups exist in most religious traditions, and the small number of such cases recounted here – while not the whole story – cannot be used to condemn the whole movement. That said, it is the case that BHIs have frequently used violent rhetoric; the divine punishment of America, mirroring that of Egypt, is a longstanding part of Black American religio-political expression. But, with the exception of NOY, such outwardly directed attacks have been extremely limited. Punishment is expected to be God's, not humans'.

We must also understand these isolated incidents in the context of the Black American experience of the time. The 1960s, 1970s, and 1980s were turbulent, anxious, and frequently violent periods when poverty and discrimination

---

[41] A small group called the Stream of Knowledge, in Albuquerque, New Mexico, appears to have attempted to form a paramilitary unit with its sights set on the Millennium – but they committed no actions and have vanished since then. They are discussed in the above reports.

pushed many families and individuals beyond what they could endure. The culmination of violence, usually internal to the groups and only occasionally directed at outsiders, was no great surprise and was a reflection of the brutality routinely experienced by Blacks in America. For some BHIs, the conviction that Black suffering was due to Black sinfulness led to a furious condemnation of any rule-breaking within their own community.

The One West BHI groups of the next section tend toward the aggressive and confrontational but have rarely ever become violent. Only a few incidents can be found, and these were always executed by lone wolves. In the most famous (and tragic) example, three people were killed in December 2019 when a man who had expressed affinity with the One West concept and ideology sprayed bullets into a kosher grocery store in Jersey City. As this case highlights, it is most often the antisemitic rhetoric which finds release through violence, and the progressive disintegration of Black–Jewish relations in the United States is a part of this although not the whole story. But those who promote narratives of hostility toward others share responsibility when those ideas become lethal.

4 Fourth Wave: Twenty-First-Century New York and Beyond

The 1980s and 1990s saw a reinvigoration of Harlem's BHI communities. The new leaders took at least as much influence from the militant and Afrocentric evolution of BHI in the Midwest and Florida. Thus a new form of BHI emerged, which was Messianic and Cultural Nationalist, but that replaced the agrarian-separatist ideals of the mid-century with an urban focus. These BHIs retained some of the restorationist impulses of the first generation while adopting a confrontational and increasingly confident public expression. Since the 1990s these groups have taken to the internet, where they appeal globally via YouTube and social media channels as well as their own websites. They are often uniquely styled, displaying a militaristic sense of identity via uniforms which designate their distinct group identity as well as appropriating Jewish and African symbols into a unique "sartorial nationalism" (Key 2023).

The founding father of the fourth wave was Edward Meredith Bibbins (1896–1972, aka Abba Bivens). Bibbins was born in Philadelphia and wed his wife Mabel in 1924; they moved to New York sometime between 1940 and 1946 and joined the Commandment Keepers. The only known writing of Bibbins, bearing his own name and that of his son, William Henry, was recently discovered (Khamr 2022). *The Marks of a Lost Race* (n.d.) was self-published in the 1940s, as a "guide to the Forty-Five Million people in America and the

British West Indies, called 'Negroes'."[42] In it, the Bibbins claim that "the Bible is the only true history of the so called Negro" (E. Bibbins & W. Bibbins n.d.). Like many discussed previously, they argue that the Gentile Age is in its last phase, and the time of unsealing the Bible is nigh. In addition, there is no known history of "the Negro" prior to 1600 – a claim technically correct, but which smuggles in the presumption that African Americans were already a people prior to their arrival in America. Indeed, one of the fundamental elements of Abba Bivens' Hebrew Israelism is that African Americans are a people distinct from all other Africans, actually closer genetically to Native Americans and other populations currently found in the Americas. Bibbins thereby radicalized Wentworth Arthur Matthew's teaching that Black Jews were descended from Jacob and white Jews from Esau. Instead, Bibbins taught that all whites were of Esau, and thus Semitic, while non-Israelite Africans were Hamitic.

The Bibbinses share Ben Ammi's assertion of a near-2,000-year period wherein scriptural truth vanished from the world; this aligns with the Gentile Age which previous Black theologians had posited as the third and final era before the redemption. The Bibbinses provide the precise dates of 70 to 1914 CE, when the gentile dispensation ended, presumably with the beginning of World War I. The Bibbinses critique "this white man who calls himself a Jew" (n.d. 13, citing Rev 2:9; 3:9), arguing that Blacks must return home, and – unusually – promote belief in the afterlife.

Edward Bibbins later recounted that he had come to awareness of the Israelite roots of Blacks and Native Americans while traveling across the country; but given some similarities in doctrine, it is not impossible that he had participated in Frank Cherry's Church of the Living God in Philadelphia. Indeed, he spent the first forty years of his life in that city. In particular, we find Cherry's thought refracted in Bibbins' apocalyptic prophecy – that in the year 2000, Christ would return and expel the white Jews from Israel.

The Bibbinses' Israelism appears to initially have been rabbinic: *Marks of a Lost Race* acknowledged the rabbinic festivals of Purim and Shemini Azeret, and a slightly later photograph shows them holding a lulav (palm frond), a distinctly rabbinic accessory for the Sukkot festival (Khamr 2022b). Bibbins Sr. attended the Commandment Keepers until 1969,[43] and while William Henry converted to Orthodox Judaism and eventually made *aliyah*, living in a religious kibbutz with his family in a West Bank settlement (Elkayam 2013), Bibbins

---

[42] The *terminus ad quem* is 1947 as it was mentioned in an interview recorded by Howard Brotz in both his monograph and his MA thesis (1947: 17).

[43] Bibbins appears in the attendance register of the Commandment Keepers – once – in 1946: Commandment Keepers records, Box 1 Folder 1.

Sr. pursued a Messianic direction, practicing the Mosaic Law while also holding that Christ is divine.[44]

After leaving the Commandment Keepers, Edward Bibbins founded his own organization, the Israeli Tanach School (ITS), at the start of the 1970s, and it is to this school that his book belongs. By this time, he was commonly known as Abba Bivens, although he had previously used the name Eber ben Yomin. The address of ITS – at One West 125th Street, Harlem – provided the informal term for Bibbins's followers and their groups: One West. This fourth wave of BHI has grown quickly from its roots in Harlem, and now many different "camps" (in their terminology), or denominations, exist across the United States, and in some cases abroad. Many of the following details were first put together by Sam Kestenbaum (2020), although Vocab Malone and Abu Khamr have also contributed much.[45]

When Abba Bivens was killed in 1973 – allegedly by some Black Muslims he had entered into debate with – two members of the school were chosen to continue his teaching. They were Masha (1924–1999) who was born Harvey Harris, but legally changed his name to Moshe ben Chareem; and Yaiqab, born Peter Sherrod, another one-time Commandment Keeper. They took over the Israeli School, rebranding it the Israeli School of Universal Practical Knowledge (ISUPK). The two, along with Yaiqab's son Ahrayah (Leonold Sherrod, b. 1939) formed the initial leadership structure, although later in the 1970s they brought in four others: the High Priests Chaazaq, Lahab, Yashiya, and Shar. Collectively they were the "Seven Heads" who ruled One West and developed an aggressive street-preaching approach. In the 1980s, they altered the name again to the Israeli Church of Universal Practical Knowledge (ICUPK), and in the late 1990s to the Israelite Church of God in Jesus Christ (ICGJC). One member broke away and continued with almost the original name – the Israelite School of Universal Practical Knowledge.

Unlike most BHIs, even those who honor Christ, ICGJC display an affinity to Christian belief by holding Christ to be divine, and accepting the virgin birth; they also preach a literal Hell. During the 1990s, member Tazadaqyah (Jermaine Grant, 1976–2020) rose through the ranks and was ultimately designated the Holy Spirit or God-sent Comforter by Ahrayah. Tazadaqyah wrested control of the ICGJC in late 2000. In 2013, ICGJC commissioned a 12-inch action figure

---

[44] Despite his son and daughter-in-law's position in HH, Bibbins himself wrote a scathing letter in June 1971, in response to their request to include his congregation in their directory, specifically rejecting any "communication with the Edomite so called Jews." Hatzaad Harishon Records, box 1 folder 3.

[45] Malone is a Calvinist Christian scholar and apologist who has spent many years studying and debating Hebrew Israelism. His major focus is One West. Khamr is an independent researcher with a longstanding interest in One West.

of Tazadaqyah, but the producers were sued as the figure was too pale. Tazadaqyah was arrested for embezzling $5 million in 2018, and died in April 2020, possibly of coronavirus. In late February 2023, Ahrahyah was reported to have died, but this was later found to be incorrect (Malone 2023).

One West underwent many splinterings. In 1995, Masha and several other members parted from Ahrayah to form the House of David, which between 1998 and 2003 split into three further schools: the Great Mill Stone (GMS, run by Tahar),[46] Israel United in Christ (IUIC, run by former police detective Nathaniel Ben Israel, b. Nathaniel Ray, 1966),[47] and House of Israel. Members of this last camp, run by Zabach, were famously present at the Lincoln Memorial confrontation between MAGA teenagers and Native Americans in 2019.[48] Further splinter groups include Lions of Israel and Gathering of Christ Church,[49] led by Rakar, which split from Philadelphia ICGJC. Almost all of these groups are based in New York but have branches in many other states. IUIC is the biggest One West camp, with tens of thousands of members and an overseas presence, while the second largest is either ICGJC or GOCC. Many other One West-influenced groups continue to appear across the Americas.[50] Those centered in New York tend to be antagonistic toward each other, often criticizing any new ideas or developments other groups adopt. One up-and-coming group is Sicarii, a splinter of GMS founded in southern California in 2012 by Ahlazar Ban Lawya (aka GRLA Hebrew, b. Adonis Gaude in Atlanta). Sicarii now has branches around the Americas and Europe.[51] On March 23, 2023, Ban Lawya publicly debated Messianic Jewish scholar Michael Brown on the identity of the modern descent of the Israelites (Berean TV 2023).

The One West camps are very similar in terms of their teachings. They largely follow in the footsteps of Abba Bivens – sections of his *Marks of a Lost Race* were incorporated into their literature into the 1990s.[52] Other than this, how-ever, the One West groups have not created any publications. They communi-cate and proselytize principally through their street and web presence. Most groups have a website and constantly active YouTube and social media

---

[46] https://greatmillstone.info/ is still online, but much more useful is the archived version at https://web.archive.org/web/20181115000000*/www.greatmillstone.info.

[47] https://israelunite.org/   [48] www.ahighergrounds.com   [49] https://gatheringofchrist.org.

[50] An occasionally updated list is at https://theshieldsquad.wordpress.com/hebrew-israelite-camps-list/ Harlem's Worldwide Truthful Understanding are discussed at length by Jackson (2005, 2013).

[51] https://sicarii.camp.

[52] An ISUPK text, *Change of World* (n.d.), claiming to have been written by Masha, Ahrayah, and Yaiqab, is in fact the first seventeen pages of *Marks of A Lost Race*, with additional material appended. This text was revised and re-edited as *Change of World's!!!* (sic) (1995) by ICUPK, with portions of *Marks* still intact.

Table 1 One West's 12 Tribes Chart

Judah	Negroes
Benjamin	West Indians
Simeon	Dominicans
Zebulon	Guatemalans & Panamanians
Ephraim	Puerto Ricans
Manasseh	Cubans
Gad	North American Indians
Reuben	Seminole Indians
Asher	Brazilians & Colombians
Naphtali	Argentinians & Chileans
Issachar	Mexicans

accounts. As a result of this, their doctrines evolve subtly and are often difficult to precisely pin down.

Apart from the now-obvious error of promoting Tazadaqyah (Jermaine Grant), Ahrayah made several important innovations which persist across the various camps. He introduced the doctrine that the KJV Bible alone is reliable, even preferable to the original Hebrew, and made the millennial return of Christ a central teaching. He received a revelation of the 12 Tribes Chart, which aligns each one of the twelve Israelite tribes with Native, enslaved, and Latin peoples across the Americas (Table 1). He also received the distinctive form of Hebrew known as Lashawan Qadash.[53] These doctrines can be seen as defining for One West BHI. While the integration of Native Americans into BHI was not uncommon and dates back to the originators, the specific aligning of all non-white Americans with Israelite tribes has allowed for a significant broadening of appeal and membership. Subsequent post-Bibbins redactions of *Marks* increasingly emphasize these others.

Vocab Malone (2017) provides ten central beliefs that One West groups conform to; an asterisk (*) indicates the belief may not be universally held:

• Blacks, Hispanics, and Native Americans who were oppressed by Europeans in the West are the true descendants of the Biblical Israelites.
• Modern Jews are impostors and not true descendants of Jacob.
• An exclusive dependence on the King James Bible (including the Apocrypha). *

---

[53] Lashawan Qadash is understood as a return to pre-Yiddish Hebrew, which is claimed to be entirely consonantal, with only two vowels – long a and i – possible in between them. The result is pronunciation entirely distinct from modern Hebrew, and virtually unusable as a spoken language. In writing, the paleo-Hebrew script is preferred.

- The imminent apocalyptic judgment of America/Europe (Edom).
- Necessity of keeping the biblical laws.
- Jesus Christ was Black.
- Gentiles cannot be saved; they are bound for death or enslavement. *
- Heaven and Hell are states of being in this world, not metaphysical realities.
- God's Name is Yahuah or Ahayah, and Jesus' name is Yahawashi or Yashayah.
- It is their duty to teach and wake the scattered Israelites to their identity.

Despite One West's dislike for whites, some groups such as GMS have attracted members of apparently white European background, arguing that because Israelite ancestry is passed solely along the paternal line, it can manifest in persons not obviously of African appearance.[54] Thus, while the racial narrative is primary to all, many groups are broadening their appeal to transcend racial exclusivity. Non-awakened Israelites are referred to as "Jakes," being short for Jacob, the name prior to the patriarch's endowment with the name Israel. The One West camps generally interpret the Semitic descent of Israel in contrast to the Hamitic descent of non-Israelite Africans, leading to a recreated racism against African Blacks. In a curious anomaly, this means that Europeans, being descended from Jacob's brother Esau, are actually Semitic, and therefore more closely related to African Americans than are Africans. In the 1995 iteration of their central text, they write, "The so-called whiteman is closer in genealogy to the 'Negro' than the African but because our people are so obsessed with the color of skin they identify with the African. The Africans are our enemies (Deut. 7:1–8) and are responsible for selling us into slavery" (Israeli Church of UPK 1995: 26). Despite this, this latest text wholly identifies whites and gentiles as, "the enemy to all nations" whose future is slavery, then "total, absolute, destruction" – a doctrine that would go on to become standard.

In addition to the 12 Tribes Chart, One West claims that their 18 Nations Table correctly associates modern nations with their biblical identity (Table 2). Thus, One West successfully manages to reduce the modern world to the biblical, creating a network of associations whereby members project themselves and the global order onto that of the Bible. Characteristics ascribed to biblical nations or their progenitors are likewise applied to their modern equivalents in ways that strain credulity (Malone 2019). Notably, the national associations are very similar to those developed by British Israelists, although the association of Edom with Turkey, i.e. the Ottomans, is replaced by Europe.

---

[54] Through some tortuous logic, and obscure single images, ICUPK argue that King James was Black (and an Israelite), as was Shakespeare, Mozart, and Beethoven. They also add Socrates, Plato, and Aristotle to the list (ICUPK 1994). Because of the belief that national identity is transmitted solely through the father, even apparent whites could in fact be Israelites, leading some to apparently apply Israelite status to anyone they respect – such as pop singer Tom Jones and actor John Travolta.

Table 2 One West's 18 Nations Table

Descendants of Japheth	
Gomer	France
Magog/Gog	Russia
Javan	Greece
Ashkenaz	Germany
Tarshish	Spain
Kittim	Italy
Descendants of Ham	
Mizraim	Egypt
Cush	Ethiopia
Phut	Libya
Canaan	South Africa
Descendants of Shem	
Elam	East Indians/Persia
Ashur	Assyria
Aram	Syria
Ishmael	Arabs
Moab	Chinese
Ammon	Japanese
Edomites	Caucasians
Jacob	Israelites

Addressing the overall One West camps by the common denominator of its previous names, Key states,

> The UPK's teachings displayed both traditional Christian elements and [. . .] traditional messianic Black Hebrew teachings. The UPK believed in the inerrancy of the 1611 King James Bible and considered it the unadulterated literal "Word of God." The Christology of the UPK was fairly traditional in most regards; they accepted the Trinity, the pre-existence of Christ, and believe in the bodily resurrection and second coming of Christ. A key difference however was the rejection of the doctrine of the virgin birth. (Key 2011: 122)

They also held some unique, idiosyncratic beliefs.

> First, the group believed in reincarnation. According to the sect, the souls of the people of the Bible continued to be recycled throughout the ages down to contemporary times. The sect asserted that their leader Masha (Moses) was actually a reincarnation of King David. Secondly, they believed UFOs were

angelic chariots. They used the descriptions given by UFO enthusiasts and cited Ezekiel's vision of the "wheel within a wheel" as proof of what people called UFOs were really "*Ma-la-ka-yam*" (angelic forces) attacking whites for their oppression of the "true" nation of Israel. (Key 2011: 122)

This interpretation of Ezekiel resembles NOI teaching. In fact, before the rifts began, One West adopted an "ancient aliens"-type doctrine about UFOs, and the role they would play in Armageddon.[55] Further bearing out the NOI influence is the racial doctrine that One Westers hold. Like some groups mentioned in the previous section, One West is separatist and believes that white Edomites are the devil. This teaching took a literal form in the NOI but is more nuanced in BHI thought, where it is usually argued that Satan has managed to infect or manipulate one part of humanity – the Edomites – into a uniquely evil position. Antisemitism has increasingly become a prominent part of this ideology, with some camps arguing that Jews are Amalekites. Generally, while all whites are held as evil, Jews represent the pinnacle of European evil, because it is they who have usurped the identity of the Black Israelites. Unlike NOI and third-wave BHI, the One West BHI does not call for geographical separation, preferring to wait for the apocalypse whereupon they shall wrest control of the Americas.

It is in these groups that we find the most coarse reading of the Hebrew Bible. The patriarchs and biblical heroes are unanimously read as mighty warriors blessed with spiritual insight and direct contact with God. These are heroic alpha males, depicted with rippling muscles, certain in their mission and without the doubt or flaws that are emphasized in Rabbinic Jewish tradition. For BHI members, an attempt to manifest those same characteristics can be seen in the wearing of bold uniform clothing, an aggressive presence and rhetoric, and a socially conservative, and extremely patriarchal, program.

Misogyny in general is common across the camps, and women are largely invisible. There are female members, but they are not publicly present, which both results from and contributes to the One West camps' heightened masculine appearance. Indeed, much of One West's posturing shares the frustrated masculinity of other internet-based movements – violent revenge fantasies against those they believe have wronged them (whites, women, Hamitic Africans); a very particular subculture and sense of humor; and clear misogyny and homophobia. Additionally, a credulous fondness for conspiracy theories has taken hold of many One Westers, leading to diatribes about the Illuminati, Freemasons, Bill Gates, and COVID vaccines, not to mention Jews. Holocaust denial – or celebration – is not uncommon (SPLC 2008; SPLC n.d.b.).

---

[55] Similar ideas were also held by the Nuwaubian Nation, a Black NRM that have absorbed NOI, Kemetic, and BHI concepts (Palmer 2010).

Despite many similarities, the camps differ from each other in important respects. IUIC is the most confident; their public presentation is accomplished, as can be seen from the professional flair of their website, flyers, and videos. GMS are the most volatile and crude, proudly displaying their resentment with all-caps typing and poor-quality graphics depicting the violent end of whites and non-Israelite Blacks, as well as violent misogyny (GMS holds a controversial doctrine that in the Messianic Age, rape of gentile women, along with any other torture and murder of gentiles, will be allowed).

Interlinked Separatisms

It has been claimed that BHI offers a mirror image of the extreme-right Christian Identity movement (ADL 1987; SPLC 2008). Several motifs are in fact shared. First, they adopt variations of the Two Seed doctrine – that Cain was sired by Satan and his lineage persists (Miller 2023c). They both have a pivotal concern with Jacob–Esau, in which Jews are the descendants of Esau. They apply Revelation 2:9 and 3:9 and its references to the Synagogue of Satan to modern Jews. They both share classical antisemitism generally, increasingly so through consecutive BHI waves. They believe in racial separatism. And they both claim to be the true Israelites. A vague interest in occult or hidden-knowledge matters is also shared, as is an expectation of imminent apocalypse which is often dealt with through rural withdrawal and self-sufficiency (Barkun 1997). Any direct influence between the two movements is impossible to prove. Wentworth Arthur Matthew had claimed Esau as the ancestor of white Jews as early as 1937, while Frank Cherry applied Revelation 2:9 and 3:9 to Jews from at least 1944; but the third and fourth waves took on a more traditional-conspiratorial antisemitism. Some of the leaders certainly absorbed antisemitism directly from customary sources – Shaleak Ben Yehuda cited both *Mein Kampf* and the *Protocols of the Elders of Zion* (1975). It is likely he also read other, less well-known, far-right religious screeds.

The BHI film *Hebrews to Negroes* (Ronald Dalton 2018), garnered much attention in 2022 after it was shared by NBA player Kyrie Irving. It was eventually removed from several streaming services because of its indulgence of a number of antisemitic tropes, including linking Jews to Cain and Satan. As well as quoting a number of white supremacist publications and the *Protocols*, the movie featured a fabricated quote from Adolf Hitler espousing BHI doctrines. The quote had been shared on social media for several years, but this represented the first broad promotion of it (Anti-Defamation League 2022).

Both Ben Yehuda and *Hebrews to Negroes* claim that Jews were in some way principal players in the transatlantic slave trade. This claim, first made in a pamphlet published by white supremacist James Konrad Warner's Sons of Liberty imprint (White 1968), was parroted by the Nation of Islam (1991), since becoming a mainstay of Black antisemitism. In addition, several reported and filmed altercations between Blacks and Jews in the United States and the United Kingdom have demonstrated that antisemitic aspects of BHI rhetoric are being used by individuals not obviously part of the movement themselves.

While antisemitism does not know any racial barriers, the comparison of BHI to Christian Identity is enlightening, because the BHI tendency to use violent rhetoric without committing actual attacks contrasts with a number of militias, violent crimes, and attempted assassinations and coups which are ascribed to Christian Identity (Schamber and Stroud 2000).

SPLC has identified ISUPK and other One West BHI as hate groups, calling them "Radical Hebrew Israelites." Certainly, One West is more radical, and more confrontational, than other groups. However, many of the fundamental beliefs are the same. As Landing argued, BHI in general formulated an early version of Black separatism and Black nationalism, and the sacred texts are identical, so perhaps the similarity is not so surprising.

5 Conclusion

The introduction claimed that BHIism represents a new form of Abrahamic religion, one that draws specifically on the Black American experience. This creative reading of the Bible through the lens of American slavery and racism has evolved over many generations, meeting the social conditions and questions arising for each. Its expansion across the globe demonstrates that the appeal is broader than simply Black America. Hebrew Israelism could be seen as yet another expression of an ongoing Israelite fixation, or even admiration, which has caused people around the globe to claim their own people are Israelites. Almost all of these movements have long since fallen out of fashion and disappeared, and the acolytes have largely moved on. Black Hebrew Israelism however is unlikely to disappear. It has persisted and steadily grown for 140 years, spreading across the globe. Dozens of different communities and congregations have been founded, and thousands, perhaps hundreds of thousands, of people are being raised within this global phenomenon, with the unshakable conviction that they are indeed Israelites. While some have and will continue to move to a closer identification with Rabbinic Judaism, as BHI becomes more established, with a longer history of its own tradition, this is likely to be less attractive. Where communities such as Respes's and Dailey's sought to enter Rabbinic Judaism, individuals seeking a more mature alternative to One West camps will be more likely to develop into members of Rabbinic BHI congregations than into Rabbinic Jews, and One West itself will likely undergo a process of maturation, and institutionalization.

Several scholars have noted the centrality of protest and resistance as a feature of BHI since it presents a method of inverting the traditional white structure of dominance, locating Blacks as the upper strata of humanity with a cosmic role and responsibility. Given this, we should recognize the specific need that BHI is fulfilling. There is a feeling on the part of many American Blacks (and Native Americans and Hispanics), that they are oppressed by a dominant power structure. BHI represents a form of resistance to this and creates unity within those oppressed segments of American society. As described, this is precisely the need that it feeds on. BHI thus represents a contemporary religion of the oppressed, a new interpretation of Abrahamic religion which draws together members of several lower-strata groups, interpreting their oppression as an ordained period of suffering that they are now leaving behind.

In the twenty-first century, many groups have taken an aggressive approach to self-promotion, but this is rooted in the originators of the movement as street preachers. For adherents, faith is not something personal between the individual and God, but something that must be spread to as many (of Israel) as possible. This is related to the communal redemption model of the movement, where the relationship is between the Israelite community and God. Because the individual is not being punished, but rather the whole, it is the whole who must return to God, and the whole who will be redeemed. Increasingly as the movement has developed, spreading the faith and "waking up" other Israelites has become the key to ending their suffering in America.

In recent times Black celebrities have expressed an affinity with BHI claims, and the idea that Black people are being punished by God is a core part of that. Kendrick Lamar's 2017 album DAMN featured BHI themes, inspired by his cousin's participation in IUIC (Kestenbaum 2020). In 2019, Nick Cannon was fired for making some classic antisemitic tropes alongside claims that Blacks were the true Jews. He responded favorably to the criticism and has since begun a podcast with ADL director Jonathan Greenblatt. Kanye West incorporated the claim that "Blacks are Jews too" into his antisemitic tirade of late 2022, while at the same Kyrie Irving tweeted a link to the film *Hebrews to Negroes*. These represent the spread of BHI thought into the mainstream, but also demonstrate the urgency with which Black, Indigenous, and People of Color in America desire an explanation for their situation, and a promise of a way out of it. Despite legal emancipation, the legacy of slavery is still keenly felt and should not be underestimated: the social position of many Black communities is perceived as a continuation of slavery and Jim Crow, despite the successes of some Blacks.

The biggest challenge to the movement is the lack of unity between groups. This is unlikely to change in the future, however, as substantial disagreements over doctrine and practice pose insurmountable boundaries. It may be that one form will achieve dominance, but this will not happen soon. Capers Funnye and the International Board of Israelite Rabbis present a likely option. However, the current reach of the One West groups suggests that a large international audience is also hungry for their approach; if they remain significant, they will necessarily undergo a process of maturation whose direction is unpredictable. It is sure that more splinters will occur, and the threat of violence going forward is not zero. Intergroup violence is likewise not impossible, and some stirrings of turf war have been seen in New York City already.

Several beliefs are shared across almost all groups. All BHIs believe that the Israelites were Black and that they, as Black Americans, are descended from them. Virtually all BHIs hold that the Mosaic Law is still relevant and that the Messianic Kingdom of God will exist in this world. Most believe that Genesis 15:13's prophecy of 400 years refers to American slavery, as does Deuteronomy 28. Most hold that Jews descend from Esau, Lost Tribes, or converts. Most believe that the apocalyptic judgment of America and the liberation of Blacks is imminent. Many understand Christianity as a form of paganism designed to entrap African slaves. In iterations that have emerged since the explosion of the NOI in the 1950s and 1960s, the teaching of whites as devils has also been a prominent feature, although this has been articulated via descent from Esau.

The explanation of slavery as a divine punishment is one of the most potent BHI doctrines. Key argued that, in his time with several congregations, he could not escape the conclusion that a "theodicy of deserved punishment" was a core theological principle (Key 2011, 2014b). Because the movement has developed either from or within the Black religious tradition, explaining the tragedy of slavery has been paramount. However, BHI has emphasized one particular mode of explanation, taking God's threats to the Israelites, present in several books of the Hebrew Bible, as prophecies which are fulfilled by the American bondage. This exegetical maneuver emerged in the 1920s at the latest and has become one of the most important aspects of Hebrew Israelism. Increasingly, as the movement has developed, the newer forms have become more focused on the teaching that Black Americans are under a curse, and that adherence to Mosaic Law is the only way to redeem themselves. Thus, where Andre Key characterized BHI's threefold agenda, it is the second that is the most salient. It is because of the understanding of the involuntary presence of Blacks in America as resulting from the curse upon Black Americans that strict adherence to the practice of Torah Law is perceived as fundamental. Without that, there can be no liberation.

However, this also serves to emphasize individual and communal agency. Human, and especially Black (Israelite) actions matter. They are what God's forgiveness depends on. This centralizing of action and personal responsibility promotes a dignity and sense of significance which can be very appealing.

It is not just the beliefs that are attractive. Many of the social features that have made previous urban religious movements popular in Black America are now drawing people to BHI. Joining and advancing in a new, localized religious movement can offer a great deal of status, respect, and responsibility. In certain disadvantaged locations, where opportunities are slim and the chance of ever really attaining a position of respect within society otherwise is unlikely, these offer an important opportunity. One Nation of Yahweh member explained her attraction to the movement, "Yesterday I had no purpose in life. Today, I am sister Israel. I'm in charge of x, y, and z" (T. Willard Fair, quoted in Amani 2007: 180).

One thing that almost all of these groups have in common is their dedication to a prophet or prophetic tradition; some even term their faith Prophetic Judaism. For virtually every group there is a foundational individual who received a divine revelation which instigated their ministry. This individual is given supreme honor in the group, and in some, each leader must be related to the originating prophet. However, the term Prophetic Judaism could also be seen to indicate the significance they place on the Bible as the record of prophecy, which, if it is not the sole scriptural authority, stands far above the respect accorded any rabbinic writings. Indeed, Prophetic Judaism could be seen as asserting the distinction of these groups from Rabbinic Judaism.

The rejection of Christianity as a slave religion developed only in the second wave, but has grown thereafter. Even for the Messianic BHI, it is an article of faith that Christianity was a distortion, a concealed paganism designed to lure the slaves away from their proper God. This belief is shared with NOI. For groups that have emerged since Black Power, it is not uncommon to reject Christianity while maintaining a belief in Christ. This is also tempered, however, with an exegesis of Psalm 82:6 and John 10:34, which applies "Ye are Gods" to all of Israel, thus making all BHIs divine, or manifesting godliness. This parallels the NOI offshoot, the Five Percenters (aka Nation of Gods and Earths) which proclaimed that every Black male is a God, and every Black female an "Earth." We might also see a similarity to Rastafari teachings about the in-dwelling God, referred to as "I and I." Thus, while these BHIs reject both Christianity and Islam as foreign incursions into African spirituality, Judaism – or rather Israelite identity – is seen as the true Black nature to which they should return.

Abbreviations

BHI   Black Hebrew Israelite/ism (depending on context)
BHIs   Black Hebrew Israelites

Black Hebrew Israelite Groups

AEI	Adath Emeth Israel
AHIJ	African Hebrew Israelites of Jerusalem
BBA	Beth B'Nai Abraham
BSBZEHC	Beth Shalom B'Nai Zaken Ethiopian Hebrew Congregation
CEH	Congregation of Ethiopian Hebrews
CK	Commandment Keepers
CLG	Church of the Living God
COGASOC	Church of God and Saints of Christ
ELNDS	Ever Live Never Die Society
GMS	Great Mill Stone
GOCC	Gathering of Christ Church
HH	Hatzaad Harishon
HOI	House of Israel
HOIHCC	House of Israel Hebrew Culture Center
HOY	House of Yisrael
ICGJC	Israelite Church of God in Jesus Christ
ICOGASOC	Independent Church of God and Saints of Christ
ICUPK	Israeli Church of Universal Practical Knowledge
ISUPK	Israeli/Israelite School of Universal Practical Knowledge
IUIC	Israel United in Christ
KOY	Kingdom of Yah
MZT	Moorish Zionist Temple
NCCI	New Covenant Congregation of Israel
NOY	Nation of Yahweh
RBAH	Righteous Branch of African Hebrews
TGK	Temple of the Gospel of the Kingdom
UEHCR	Union of Ethiopian Hebrew Congregations and Rabbis

Non-BHI Groups

COGIC	Church of God in Christ
MST	Moorish Science Temple
NOI	Nation of Islam

References

Primary Sources

Ammi, B. (1982). *God, the Black Man, and Truth*. Washington, DC: Communicators Press.

Ben Levi, C. M. (1997). *Israelites and Jews: The Significant Difference*. Kearney, NE: Morris.

Ben Levy, Rabbi S. (n.d.a). The Destruction of Commandment Keepers, Inc. 1919–2007. www.blackjews.org/Essays/DestructionofCommandmentKeepers .html.

Ben Levy, Rabbi S. (n.d.b). Biography of Rabbi Yirmeyahu Israel / History of Kohol Beth B'nai Yisrael and Bnai Adath Kol Bet Yisrael. www.blackjews .org/rabbi-yirmeyahu-israel/.

Ben Levy, Rabbi S. (n.d.c). Cohen Levi Ben Yisrael: His Life and Legacy. www .blackjews.org/biography-of-cohen-levi-yisrael/.

Ben Levy, Rabbi S. (n.d.d). Biography of Rabbi Levi Ben Levy / History of Beth Shalom and Beth Elohim. www.blackjews.org/biography-of-rabbi-levi-ben-levy/.

Ben Levy, Rabbi S. (n.d.e). Dr. Rudolph Windsor: Griot of His People. http:// blackjews.org/Essays/Rudolph%20Windsor%20Griot%20of%20His% 20People.pdf.

Ben Levy, Rabbi S. (n.d.f). Rabbi Robert Devine. www.blackjews.org/rabbi-robert-devine/.

Ben Levy, Rabbi S. (n.d.g). Reflections on Rabbi W. A. Matthew. www.black jews.org/Essays/Reflections%20on%20Rabbi%20W.A.%20Matthew.pdf.

Ben Levy, Rabbi S. (n.d.h). Who Are We? Where Did We Come From? How Many of Us Are There? www.blackjews.org/articles.htm.

Ben Yehuda, S. (1975). *Black Hebrew Israelites from America to the Promised Land: The Great International Religious Conspiracy against the Children of the Prophets*. New York: Vantage Press.

Berean TV. (2023). Who Are the Real Children of Israel Debate? *YouTube*. www.youtube.com/watch?v=4uGyKVBLUW0.

Beth Shalom B'nai Zaken EHC. (n.d.). *Our History*. https://bethshalombz.org/ history.

Bibbins, W. H. & E. (n.d.). *Marks of a Lost Race*. New York: W. H. & E. Bibbins.

Chakwal Morton Cragg Papers. (n.d.). SC-08792. The Jacob Rader Marcus Center of the American Jewish Archives. Cincinnati, OH: Hebrew Union College.

Chatwick, G. A. (1974). *The Lost Nation (The So Called "Negro")*. Philadelphia, PA: Culture Craft for Beth Hephzibah.

Christian, W. (1896). *Poor Pilgrim's Work, in the Name of Father, Son and Holy Ghost on Christian Friendship Works*. Texarkana, AR: Joe Erlich's Printing.

Church of God and Saints of Christ Temple Beth El. (n.d.). *Chief Bishop Joseph W. Crowdy*. www.cogasoc.org/leaders/chief-bishop-joseph-w-crowdy/.

Commandment Keepers Ethiopian Hebrew Congregation records (1996). Sc MG 574. Schomburg Center for Research in Black Culture, New York Public Library.

Cook, Bishop A. W. (1925). *The Independent Church of God of the Juda Tribe of Israel: The Black Jews*. New York: A. W. Cook.

Crowdy, Bishop W. S. (1902). *The Revelation of God Revealed*. Philadelphia, PA: Church of God Publication House.

Dalton, R. Jr. (2018). *Hebrews to Negroes: Wake up Black America*. 208 minutes. The Negro Network.

Emmanuel, T. (1955). Letter to Chakwal Cragg. (Chakwal Morton Cragg Papers, Box 1 Folder 1).

Hatzaad Harishon Records. Sc MG 576. Schomburg Center for Research in Black Culture, New York Public Library.

Israel, M. (1981). *You Are Not a Nigger: Our True History, the World's Best Kept Secret*. Hollywood, FL: Nation of Yahweh.

Israeli School of UPK. (n.d.). *Change of World*. New York: ISUPK.

Lewi, U. (2009). *Interview Brother Azriel Devine*. YouTube. www.youtube.com/watch?v=wBRRucEgPjk.

Nation of Islam. (1991). *The Secret Relationship between Blacks and Jews*, vol. 1. Boston, MA: Nation of Islam.

Nation of Yahweh collection. 176. Amistad Research Center. Tulane University.

Nation of Yahweh. (n.d.). *The War in Heaven*. www.yahwehbenyahweh.com/Operation_Word_War/pdf/Operation_Word_War_Web.pdf.

Porter, S. (1990). *The Truth, the Lies, and the Bible*. Toronto: Fifth RIbb.

Respes, A. (1971). Letter to the Editor. *Philadelphia Jewish Exponent*. November 5, p. 36.

The Israeli Church of UPK. (1995). *Change of World's!!!* [sic]. New York: ICUPK.

The Israelite Church of UPK. (1994). *Images of Israel in History*. New York: ICUPK.

Weaver, D. (n.d.). *Biography of Rabbi Dahton Nasi.* www.blackjews.org/rabbi-dahton-nasi-a-zadek-remembered/.

White, W. (1968). *Who Brought the Slaves to America? Slavery and the Jews.* Hollywood, CA: Western Front and Metairie, LA: Sons of Liberty.

Windsor, R. (1969). *From Babylon to Timbuktu: A History of the Ancient Black Races Including the Black Hebrews.* Atlanta, GA: Windsor's Golden Series.

YisraEL, M. E. (2014). *Setting the Crooked Things Straight: The Teaching of Yah's Prophet.* Cincinnati, OH: World Ingathering of the Children of YisraEL.

Secondary Sources

Africology: Journal of Pan-African Studies 8.10 (2016) Special Issue on Yosef A. A. ben Jochannan

Amani, K. (2007). *My Id . . . Ignant & Dissfunkshunal! Life in the Yahweh Cult and the Witness Protection Program: A Memoir.* New York: iUniverse.

Anti-Defamation League. (1987). *Research Report: The Black Hebrew Israelites.* New York: Anti-Defamation League of B'nai B'rith.

Anti-Defamation League. (2022). Hebrews to Negroes: What you Need to Know. *ADL Blog*, November 3. www.adl.org/resources/blog/hebrews-negroes-what-you-need-know.

Atlanta Constitution. (1926). Shriners from Arabia Denied Lodging because of Color. June 11.

Baptista, T. (2019). *The Flamingos: A Complete History of the Doo-Wop Legends.* Jefferson, NC: MacFarland.

Barkun, M. (1997). *Religion and the Racist Right: The Origins of the Christian Identity Movement*, rev ed. Chapel Hill, NC: University of North Carolina Press.

Ben-Jochannan, Y. A. A. (1993; 1983). *We the Black Jews: Witness to the "White Jewish Race" Myth.* Baltimore, MD: Black Classic Press.

Ben-Ur, A. (2020). *Jewish Autonomy in a Slave Society: Suriname in the Atlantic World, 1651–1825.* Philadelphia, PA: University of Pennsylvania Press.

Berry, J. C. (1977). Black Jews: A Study of Status Malintegration and (Multi) Marginality. PhD dissertation, Syracuse University.

Blythe, J. (1989). A Dream Deferred. *The Paducah Sun.* September 24, p. 1, 4; September 25, p. 1, 12; September 26, p. 10.

Bollman, T. (2018). The Bible and Black Identity: Israel United in Christ and the Hebrew Israelite Movement. MA thesis, Indiana University.

Bowles, B. (1983). Troubled Life: "Prophet" Talks about His Faith. *Detroit Free Press*, July 13, p. 3.

Brotz, H. (1947). The Black Jews of Harlem. MA thesis, University of Chicago.

Brotz, H. M. (1964). *The Black Jews of Harlem: Negro Nationalism and the Dilemmas of Negro Leadership*. London: Free Press of Glencoe.

Bruder, E. (2008). *The Black Jews of Africa: History, Identity, Religion*. Oxford: Oxford University Press.

Bruder, E., and Parfitt, T. (2012). *African Zion: Studies in Black Judaism*. Newcastle: Cambridge Scholars.

Chester, H. (1974). The Black Rabbi Pays Milwaukee a Visit. *Jewish Post & Opinion*, February 22, pp. 17–18, 31.

Chireau, Y., and Deutsch N. (2000). *Black Zion: African American Religious Encounters with Judaism*. New York: Oxford University Press.

Cogswell, L. (1981). Black "Prophet" Calls Negro His Enemy. *The Herald Palladium*, April 25, p. 1.

Cohen, W. (1965). Community Welcomes Black Jews. *Jewish Post* (Indianapolis), September 3, pp. 3–4, 14.

Crawford, M. N. (2006). Natural Black Beauty and Black Drag. In L. G. Collins and M. N. Crawford, eds., *New Thoughts on the Black Arts Movement*, New Brunswick: Rutgers University Press, pp. 154–73.

Dorman, J. S. (2004). The Black Israelites of Harlem and the Professors of Oriental and African Mystic Science in the 1920's. PhD dissertation, University of California, Los Angeles.

Dorman, J. S. (2012). A Colony in Babylon: Cooperation and Conflict between Black and White Jews in New York, 1930 to 1964. In E. Bruder and T. Parfitt, eds., *African Zion: Studies in Black Judaism*. Newcastle upon Tyne: Cambridge Scholars, pp. 220–33.

Dorman, J. S. (2013). *Chosen People: The Rise of American Black Israelite Religions*. Oxford: Oxford University Press.

E. E. (2020). Jews of Color in America: Yasminah Respes's Story. *YouTube*. www .youtube.com/watch?v=d7KUj8Nwzpk&list=PLLnzqfgSuU5E3_gwigJXcQm TX4jKOrNg0.

Eliade, M. (1959). *The Sacred and the Profane: The Nature of Religion*. New York: Houghton Miflin Harcourt.

Elkayam, L. (2013). Departures Arrivals: Haim Bibbins Becomes a New Arrival at 86. *HaAretz*, May 30. www.haaretz.com/2013-05-30/ty-article/ .premium/departures-arrivals-haim-bibbins-becomes-a-new-immigrant-at-86/0000017f-efb2-d223-a97f-efff73730000.

Emre, M. (2017). How a Fictional Racist Plot Made the Headlines and Revealed an American Truth. *The New Yorker*, December 31. www.newyorker.com/ books/second-read/how-a-fictional-racist-plot-made-the-headlines-and-revealed-an-american-truth.

Esensten, A. (2019). Yah's Exemplary Soldiers: African Hebrew Israelites in the Israel Defense Forces. *Religions*, 10.11. www.mdpi.com/2077-1444/10/11/614.

Fauset, A. H. (2001; 1944). *Black Gods of the Metropolis: Negro Religious Cults of the Urban North.* Philadelphia, PA: University of Pennsylvania Press.

FBI. (1968). Cointelpro Memorandum, March 3. https://archive.org/details/FBI-Neutralize-King/1968-03-04-COINTELPRO/mode/2up.

FBI. (1999). *Project Megiddo.* www.fbi.gov:80/library/megiddo/publicmegiddo.pdf.

Fernheimer, J. W. (2012). Leading through Listening: Racial Tensions in 1968 New York. In E. Bruder and T. Parfitt, eds., *African Zion: Studies in Black Judaism*, Newcastle upon Tyne: Cambridge Scholars, pp. 234–62.

Fernheimer, J. W. (2014). *Stepping into Zion: Hatzaad Harishon, Black Jews, and the Remaking of Jewish Identity.* Tuscaloosa, AL: The University of Alabama Press.

Frazier, N. (2012). The "Other" Jim Jones: Rabbi David Hill, House of Israel, and Black American Religion in the Age of Peoples Temple. *The Jonestown Report* 14. https://jonestown.sdsu.edu/?page_id=34259.

Frazier, N. (n.d.). Oral History Interview with Dick Peery. *Harambee City.* https://harambeecity.lib.miamioh.edu/items/show/78.

Freedberg, S. P. (1994). *Brother Love: Murder, Money, and a Messiah.* New York: Pantheon Books.

Fulop, T. E. (1991). "The Future Golden Day of the Race": Millennialism and Black Americans in the Nadir, 1877–1901. *Harvard Theological Review*, 84.1, 75–99.

Gelman, M. (1965). Adat Beyt Moshe – The Colored House of Moses, A Study of the Contemporary Negro Religious Community and Its Leader. PhD dissertation, University of Pennsylvania.

George, J. (2008). Promised Land, Promise Fading. *Chicago Tribune*, July 7.

Gillick, J. (2009). Post-Racial Rabbis. *Moment*, July–August. https://momentmag.com/post-racial-rabbis-2/5/.

Guyana Chronicle. (2014). Corbin Delivered Guns to House of Israel. June 3. https://guyanachronicle.com/2014/06/03/corbin-delivered-guns-to-house-of-israel/.

Haynes, B. D. (2018). *The Soul of Judaism: Jews of African Descent in America.* New York: New York University Press.

Hernandez, T. H. (1932). To Heaven, Dead or Alive: Rare Religion Believes in Immortality. *The Pittsburgh Courier*, July 30, p. 13.

Isaac, W. (2006). Locating Afro-American Judaism: A Critique of White Normativity. In J. A. Gordon and L. R. Gordon, eds., *The Companion to African American Studies*, Oxford: Blackwell, pp. 512–42.

Isaac, W. (2012). Beyond Ontological Jewishness: A Philosophical Reflection on the Study of African American Jews and the Social Problems of the Jewish and Human Sciences. PhD dissertation, Temple University.

Jackson Jr., J. L. (2005). *Real Black: Adventures in Racial Sincerity*. Chicago, IL: University of Chicago Press.

Jackson Jr., J. L. (2013). *Thin Description: Ethnography and the African Hebrew Israelites of Jerusalem*. Cambridge, MA: Harvard University Press.

Kaye/Kantrowitz, M. (2007). *The Colors of Jews: Racial Politics and Radical Diasporism*. Bloomington: Indiana University Press.

Kestenbaum, S. (2014). Rabbi Hailu Moshe Paris, Revered Leader of America's Black Jews, Dies at 81. *Forward*, November 6. https://forward.com/news/208669/rabbi-hailu-moshe-paris-revered-leader-of-americas/.

Kestenbaum, S. (2015). Can This Rabbinic Revolutionary Make Hebrew Israelites Mainstream? *Forward*, July 7. https://forward.com/news/311361/can-rabbinic-revolutionary-capers-funnye-push-hebrew-israelites-into/.

Kestenbaum, S. (2016). On Jerusalem Walls, Artist Memorializes Black Rabbi from Harlem. *Forward*, March 31. https://forward.com/schmooze/337231/on-jerusalem-walls-artist-memorializes-black-rabbi-from-harlem/.

Kestenbaum, S. (2020). "I'm an Israelite": Kendrick Lamar's Spiritual Search, Hebrew Israelite Religion, and the Politics of a Celebrity Encounter. In C. M. Driscoll, A. B. Pinn, and M. R. Miller, eds., *Kendrick Lamar and the Making of Black Meaning*, Oxon: Routledge, 16.

Key, A. E. (2011). What's My Name? An Autoethnography of the Problem of Moral Evil and Ethnic Suffering in Black Judaism. PhD dissertation, Temple University.

Key, A. E. (2014a). Toward a Typology of Black Hebrew Religious thought and Practice. *Journal of Africana Religions*, 2.1, 31–66.

Key, A. E. (2014b). If thou Do Not Hearken unto the Voice of the Lord thy God: A Critique of Theodicy in Black Judaism. *Black Theology*, 12.3, 267–88.

Key, A. E. (2023a). Did You Read about Conservative Judaism's Anti-Black Antisemitic Smearing of Hebrew Israelites? Neither Did I. *Religion Dispatches*, March 7. https://religiondispatches.org/did-you-read-about-conservative-judaisms-anti-black-antisemitic-smearing-of-hebrew-israelites-neither-did-i/.

Key, A. E. Brooks. (2023b). Holy Dashikis! Black Sartorial Nationalism and Black Israelite Religion. In M. W. Dallam and B. E. Zeller, eds., *Religion,*

Attire, and Adornment in North America, New York: Columbia University Press, pp. 117–42.

Khamr, A. (2022a). Abba Bibins' Book? *YouTube*. www.youtube.com/watch? v=aOp3G7xcEvY.

Khamr, A. (2022b). Insights on the Photo of Ahrayah & Bibbins. *YouTube*. www.youtube.com/watch?v=FWnwimcTGVc.

Koppel, N. (2008). Black Rabbi Reaches out to Mainstream of His Faith. *New York Times*, March 16. www.nytimes.com/2008/03/16/us/16rabbi.html.

Landing, J. (2002). *Black Judaism: Story of an American Movement*. Durham, NC: Carolina Academic Press.

Leibman, L. A. (2021). *Once We Were Slaves: The Extraordinary Journey of a Multiracial Jewish Family*. Oxford: Oxford University Press.

LifeWay Research. (2019). African American Attitudes toward Israel. http:// lwresearch21.wpengine.com/wp-content/uploads/2019/11/The-Philos-Project-African-American-Attitudes-Toward-Israel-Report.pdf.

Lis, D., Miles, W. F. S., and Parfitt T. (2016). *In the Shadow of Moses: New Jewish Movements in Africa and the Diaspora*. Los Angeles: African Academic Press.

Lyons, L. (2014). Losing a Gentle Lion of Judah: Remembering Rabbi Hailu Moshe Paris, Spiritual Leader of Black Jewry. *Tablet*, November 14. www .tabletmag.com/sections/news/articles/losing-a-gentle-lion-of-judah.

Malone, V. (2017). *Barack Obama Vs The Black Hebrew Israelites: Introduction to the History & Beliefs of 1West Israelism*. Phoenix, AZ: Thureos.

Malone, V. (2019). Why Do 1West "Hebrew Israelites" Call Whites "Edomites" and Chinese "Moabites"? *Christian Research Journal*. www.equip.org/art icles/why-do-1west-hebrew-israelites-call-whites-edomites-and-chinese-moabites/.

Malone, V. (2023). The AHRAYAH/MASHA Split – 90s 1Wester Tells the Story. *YouTube*. www.youtube.com/watch?v=pCZzNBaK83s&t=984s.

ManIshtana. (2012). *Thoughts from a Unicorn: 100% Black. 100% Jewish. 0% Safe*. New York: Hyphen.

Markowitz, F. (1996). Israel as Africa, Africa as Israel: "Divine Geography" in the Personal Narratives and Community Identity of the Black Hebrew Israelites. *Anthropological Quarterly*, 69.4, 193–205.

Markowitz, F. (2000). Millenarian Motherhood: Motives, Meanings and Practices among African Hebrew Israelite Women. *Nashim: A Journal of Jewish Women's Studies & Gender Issues*, 3, 106–38.

Markowitz, F., and Avieli, N. (2020). Food for the Body and Soul: Veganism, Righteous Male Bodies, and Culinary Redemption in the Kingdom of Yah. *Ethnography*, 23.2, 181–203.

Markowitz, F., Helman, S., and Shir-Vertesh, D. (2003). Soul Citizenship: The Black Hebrews and the State of Israel. *American Anthropologist*, 105.2, 302–12.

Michaeli, E. (2000). Another Exodus: The Hebrew Israelites from Chicago to Dimona. In Y. Chireau and N. Deutsch, eds., *Black Zion: African American Religious Encounters with Judaism*, New York: Oxford University Press, pp. 73–90.

Miller, M. T. (2023a). Ben Ammi's Adaptation of Veganism in the Theology of the African Hebrew Israelites. *Interdisciplinary Journal for Religion and Transformation in Contemporary Society*, 9.2, 417–44.

Miller, M. T. (2023b). Bishop Allan Wilson Cook (Rabbi Haling Hank Lenht), Queen Malinda Morris, and the Independent Church of God: A Missing Piece in the History of Hebrew Israelite Black Judaism. *Black Theology*, 23.1, 257–74.

Miller, M. T. (2023c). *Ben Ammi Ben Israel: Black Theology, Theodicy, and Judaism in the thought of the African Hebrew Israelite Messiah*. London: Bloomsbury.

Mock, B. (2007). Nation of Yahweh Mourns Loss of Leader, Shows Signs of New Life. *Southern Poverty Law Center Intelligence Report*, Fall 2007. www.splcenter.org/fighting-hate/intelligence-report/2007/nation-yahweh-mourns-loss-leader-shows-signs-new-life.

Murphy, J. (1980). Israelite Community near Ullin Waits out the Coming Armageddon. *Southern Illinoisan*, August 4, p. 18.

Naval Criminal Investigative Service. (1999). Anti-Government Extremists: An Information Project. August 1999. https://ncisahistory.org/wp-content/uploads/2018/07/NCIS-Anti-Government-Extremist-Study-Aug1999.pdf.

New York Age. (1921). "Live Ever, Never Die" Prophet Runs Amuck. July 2, pp. 1–2.

New York Times. (1974). Gangs Terrorizing Brooklyn Merchants. February 25, p. 1.

Palmer, S. (2010). *The Nuwaubian Nation: Black Spirituality and State Control*. Burlington, VT: Ashgate.

Parfitt, T. (2020). *Hybrid Hate: Conflations of Antisemitism & Anti-Black Racism from the Renaissance to the Third Reich*. New York: Oxford University Press.

Parfitt, T., and Semi, E. T. (2002). *Judaising Movements: Studies in the Margins of Judaism*. Oxon: Routledge.

Perkins, K. (1983). "True Jews" Prepare for Armageddon. *Daily Egyptian*, February 11, p. 5.

Pew Research Center. (2013). *A Portrait of Jewish Americans: Findings from a Pew Research Center Survey of U.S. Jews.* www.pewresearch.org/religion/wp-content/uploads/sites/7/2013/10/jewish-american-survey-full-report.pdf.

Podcast against Antisemitism. (2023). "No Shame or Fear," with Tova the Poet. *Podcast against Antisemitism,* 3.20. https://antisemitism.org/podcast/#listen.

Raboteau, A. J. (1995). *A Fire in the Bones: Reflections on African-American Religious History.* Boston: Beacon Press.

Raboteau, A. J. (1978). *Slave Religion: The "Invisible Institution" in the Antebellum South.* Updated Edition. Oxford: Oxford University Press.

Rogers, J. A. (1968; 1940). *Sex and Race: Negro-Caucasian Mixing in All Ages and All Lands.* St. Petersburg, FL: Helga M Rogers.

Rosenzweig, A. (1963). Black Jews of South Side. *Chicago Defender,* February 2, pp. 1–2.

Ross, D. (2009). Jew Like Me: An Oral History of Congregation Temple Bethel, a Black Synagogue in the West Oak Lane Neighborhood of Philadelphia. *Undergraduate Humanities Forum 2008–2009: Change.* 4. http://repository.upenn.edu/uhf_2009/4 and the source interviews online, Black Hebrews at Temple Bethel Congregation. *National Library of Israel.* www.nli.org.il, www.bethel-ph.org/.

Rubel, N. L. (2009). Chased out of Palestine: Prophet Cherry's Church of God and Early Black Judaisms in the United States. In E. E. Curtis and D. B. Sigler, eds., *The New Black Gods: Arthur Huff Fauset and the Study of African American Religions,* Bloomington: Indiana University Press, pp. 49–69.

Sapoznik, H. (2020). How European Jews Saw the African American Cantor. www.henrysapoznik.com/post/how-european-jews-saw-the-african-american-cantor-the-1930-toyve-ha-cohen-tour.

Sapulkas, A. (1974). Follower of Chenault Says Present-Day Events Are All Explained in the Bible. *New York Times,* July 9, p. 17.

Schamber, J. F., and Stroud, S. R. (2000). Mystical Anti-Semitism and the Christian Identity Movement: A Narrative Criticism of Dan Gayman's "The Two Seeds of Genesis 3:15." Paper presented at the Annual Meeting of the National Communication Association, November 9–12.

Semi, E. T. (2016). *Taamrat Emmanuel: An Ethiopian Jewish Intellectual, between Colonized and Colonizers.* New York: Centro Primo Levi.

Singer, M. (2000). Symbolic Identity Formation in an African American Religious Sect: The Black Hebrew Israelites. In Y. Chireau and N. Deutsch, eds., *Black Zion: African American Religious Encounters with Judaism,* New York: Oxford University Press, pp. 55–72.

Southern Illinoisan. (1983). Awaiting Armageddon. July 10, pp. 31–32.

Southern Poverty Law Center. (1997). Rough Waters: Stream of Knowledge Probed by Officials. *Intelligence Report*. Fall 1997.Southern Poverty Law Center. (2008). Racist Black Hebrew Israelites Becoming more Militant. *Intelligence Report*, August 29. www.splcenter.org/fighting-hate/intelli gence-report/2008/racist-black-hebrew-israelites-becoming-more-militant.

Southern Poverty Law Center. (n.d.a). HQ-1. p. 28. https://archive.org/details/ SouthernPovertyLawCenterHQ1.

Southern Poverty Law Center. (n.d.b). Radical Hebrew Israelites. www.splcen ter.org/fighting-hate/extremist-files/group/radical-hebrew-israelites.

Srole, I. (1978). Inner City Santuary: The History and Theology of Rochester's Black Jews. MA thesis, Rochester Institute of Technology.

Standish, F. (1983). "Truth" Hit "Prophet" after Stint in Army. *The South Bend Tribune*, July 11, p. 16.

Stewart, C. O. (1966). Religious Group to Await God in Southern Illinois Camp. *Southern Illinoisan*, May 29, p. 32.

Sznajderman, M. (1985). "Prophet" Wants His People Airlifted from Here to Israel. *Alabama Journal*, January 21, p. 2.

The Broad Ax. (1926). Slave Ring is Revealed under Guise of Cult. February 20, p. 2.

The Pittsburgh Courier. (1967). Negro Tied in Bible Prophecy. August 5, p. 3.

The Washington Post. (1906). Prophet Crowdy Causes Consternation. January 28, p. 8.

Van Bennekom. P. (1979). American Leading New Cult in Guyana. *Daily Vidette*, November 27, pp. 1–9.

Warmbrand, M. J. (1969). Black Jews of America. *The Hourglass*, 1.2, 86–106.

Williams, J. J. (1930). *Hebrewisms of West Africa: From Nile to Niger with the Jews*. London: Allen & Unwin.

Willis, S. M. (2021). The House of Yisrael Cincinnati: How Normalized Institutional Violence Can Produce a Culture of Unorthodox Resistance 1963 to 2021. MA thesis, Wright State University.

Wisconsin Jewish Herald. (1973). Black Israelites Impress Shalom. February 9, p. 2.

Yette, S. F. (1971). *The Choice: The Issue of Black Survival in America*. New York: GP Putnam's.

Young, M. (1961). They're Talking about. *Call and Post*, February 11, p. 19.

Zihiri, S. (2020). Ambassadors of Christ and Israel United in Christ: Comparing the Preaching Strategies of Black Hebrew Israelite Camps. *UCLA Journal of Religion*, 4, 30–68.

Cambridge Elements ≡

New Religious Movements

Founding Editor
†James R. Lewis
Wuhan University
The late James R. Lewis was Professor of Philosophy at Wuhan University, China.
He served as the editor or co-editor for four book series, was the general editor for the
Alternative Spirituality and Religion Review, and the associate editor for the *Journal of
Religion and Violence*. His publications include *The Cambridge Companion to Religion and
Terrorism* (Cambridge University Press 2017) and *Falun Gong: Spiritual Warfare and
Martyrdom* (Cambridge University Press 2018).

Series Editor
Rebecca Moore
San Diego State University
Rebecca Moore is Emerita Professor of Religious Studies at San Diego State
University. She has written and edited numerous books and articles on Peoples Temple and
the Jonestown tragedy. She has served as co-general editor or reviews editor of *Nova
Religio* since 2000. Publications include *Beyond Brainwashing: Perspectives on Cult Violence*
(Cambridge University Press 2018) and *Peoples Temple and Jonestown in the Twenty-First
Century* (Cambridge University Press 2022).

About the Series
Elements in New Religious Movements go beyond cult stereotypes and popular
prejudices to present new religions and their adherents in a scholarly and engaging
manner. Case studies of individual groups, such as Transcendental Meditation and
Scientology, provide in-depth consideration of some of the most well known, and
controversial, groups. Thematic examinations of women, children, science, technology,
and other topics focus on specific issues unique to these groups. Historical analyses
locate new religions in specific religious, social, political, and cultural contexts. These
examinations demonstrate why some groups exist in tension with the wider society and
why others live peaceably in the mainstream. The series highlights the differences, as well
as the similarities, within this great variety of religious expressions. To discuss
contributing to this series please contact Professor Moore, remoore@sdsu.edu.

Cambridge Elements ≡

New Religious Movements

Elements in the Series

Printed in the United States
by Baker & Taylor Publisher Services